Keswick: A Bibliographic Introduction to the Higher Life Movement

by

David Bundy

Occasional Bibliographic Papers of the B.L. Fisher

Library #3

First Fruits Press
Wilmore, Kentucky
c2012

asburyseminary.edu
800.2ASBURY
204 North Lexington Avenue
Wilmore, Kentucky 40390

First Fruits
THE ACADEMIC OPEN PRESS OF ASBURY SEMINARY

ISBN: 9780984738632

Keswick: a Bibliographic Introduction to the Higher Life Movements, by
David D. Bundy.
First Fruits Press, © 2012
B. L. Fisher Library, Asbury Theological Seminary, © 1975

Digital version at http://place.asburyseminary.edu/firstfruitspapers/2/

Bundy, David D.
    Keswick : a bibliographic introduction to the higher life movements / by David D.
    Bundy.
    Wilmore, Ky. : First Fruits Press, c2012.
    89 p. ; 21 cm. -- (Occasional bibliographic papers of the B. L. Fisher Library ;
    no. 3)
    Reprint. Previously published: Wilmore, Ky. : B.L. Fisher Library, Asbury
    Theological Seminary, c1975.
    ISBN 9780984738632 (pbk.)
    1. Keswick movement -- Bibliography. I. Title. II. B. L. Fisher Library. Occasional
    papers ; no. 3.
    Z7776.5 .B8 2012

Cover design by Haley Hill

asburyseminary.edu
800.2ASBURY
204 North Lexington Avenue
Wilmore, Kentucky 40390

First Fruits
THE ACADEMIC OPEN PRESS OF ASBURY SEMINARY

KESWICK:

A BIBLIOGRAPHIC INTRODUCTION

TO

THE HIGHER LIFE MOVEMENTS

KESWICK:

A BIBLIOGRAPHIC INTRODUCTION

TO

THE HIGHER LIFE MOVEMENTS

by

David D. Bundy

The Third in a Series of
"Occasional Bibliographic Papers
of the B. L. Fisher Library"

B. L. Fisher Library
Asbury Theological Seminary
Wilmore, Kentucky 40390
1975

Occasional Bibliographic Papers of the
B. L. Fisher Library:

No. 1.   The American Holiness Movement; a
          Bibliographic Introduction. Donald
          W. Dayton. 1971. 59 p. $2.00.
          Out-of-print. New edition in process.

No. 2.   The American Pentecostal Movement; a
          Bibliographic Essay. David W. Faupel.
          1972. 56 p. $2.00.

No. 3.   Keswick: a Bibliographic Introduc-
          tion to the Higher Life Movements.
          David D. Bundy. 1975. 89 p. $3.00.

Order Information

Prices listed above for 1 - 10 copies. For
11 or more copies the price per copy is re-
duced by fifty cents ($0.50) plus postage and
handling unless payment accompanies order.

ISBN 0-914368-03-6

Address:

          Director of Library Services
          B. L. Fisher Library
          Asbury Theological Seminary
          Wilmore, Ky. 40390

PREFACE

This third monograph in the series, "Occasional Bibliographic Papers of the B. L. Fisher Library" follows Donald W. Dayton's THE AMERICAN HOLINESS MOVEMENT: A BIBLIOGRAPHIC INTRODUCTION and David W. Faupel's THE AMERICAN PENTECOSTAL MOVEMENT, A BIBLIOGRAPHICAL ESSAY, at the suggestion of Dr. Melvin Dieter.

I wish to express appreciation to Dr. Susan A. Schultz, Director of the B. L. Fisher Library of Asbury Theological Seminary, for her patient encouragement throughout the duration of the project and for her critical evaluation of the manuscript.

A special debt of gratitude is owed to the persons who in responding to the first draft of this essay saved me from a multitiude of errors and provided suggestions from the areas of their expertise: Dr. James Hamilton, Asbury College, has a prodigious knowledge of nineteenth century America and England; Dr. Melvin Dieter, Director of Wesleyan Educational Institutions, and Mr. Donald W. Dayton, Director of Mellander Library and Assistant Professor of Theology at North Park Theological Seminary, are thoroughly aware of the literature and history of the European "Higher Life" Movements and the American Holiness Movement; Mr. David W. Faupel, Assistant Professor of Bibliography and Research at Asbury Theological Seminary has special expertise with regard to the literature of Pentecostalism and has continually provided insights and encouragement during the evolution of this essay; Dr. J. Edwin Orr graciously provided suggestions incorporated herein. I alone accept responsibility for any errors which may remain, and would appreciate information on any inaccuracy discovered by the readers.

I am also grateful for access to several excellent collections and to the unfailing generosity and kind helpfulness of librarians and their staff assistants: Garrett-Evangelical Seminary; Moody Bible Institute; The Southern Baptist Theological Seminary; The Regenstein Library; The University of Chicago; and especially the B. L. Fisher Library, Asbury Theological Seminary. Access to the personal collections of Dr. James Hamilton and Mr. Donald W. Dayton provided materials which filled serious lacunae in my research.

Finally, I wish to express my sincere thanks to Mrs. Joan Smith, Mrs. Wendy Ferns and Mrs. Kris Cryderman who cheerfully and accurately typed from manuscripts that were usually difficult, to Mrs. Gilbert (Esther) James who with patient persistence edited the text and verified bibliographic entries, and to Mrs. Linda Gates who prepared the final copy for printing.

One further word of explanation is due. For historic purposes the publication dates for titles listed are the earliest that could be established, and for brevity's sake, normally, only one publisher is cited. Many of these titles were published on both sides of the Atlantic; many reprints were issued. Please consult both the U. S. and British BOOKS-IN-PRINT for current publication data.

David D. Bundy
Instructor in Greek
Asbury Theological Seminary

* As of September 1, 1975, Dr. Dieter is Associate Professor of Church History, Asbury Theological Seminary.

Contents

Preface   5

Introduction and Definition   9

History and Influence of Keswick   10

  Setting the Stage   10

  Histories of Keswick   24

  Influence of Keswick   28

      The Welsh Revival   28
      The German Holiness Movement   30
      Foreign Missions   32
      Conventions Abroad   35
      The American Holiness Movement   42
      The American Pentecostal Movement   47
      The Christian and Missionary Alliance   49

Literature of Keswick   52

  Bibliography   53

  Theological Studies   53

  Biblical Studies   70

  Sermonic and Devotional Studies   75

  Hymnody   80

  Periodicals   81

Index   85

INTRODUCTION AND DEFINITION

A difficult problem in attempting to prepare
an introduction to the literature of the Keswick Movement is the matter of definition.
Keswick, a small town in northwest England,
has since 1875 been the site of the famed
Keswick Convention. The Keswick Convention
is not a denomination. It has no membership
rolls. Nor does Keswick have a precisely de-
limited tradition. The Keswick Convention
is, instead, an amorphous conglomerate of in-
dividuals and groups who are in sympathy with
the teachings and lifestyle as taught at the
annual meeting and proclaimed in the official
record of the Keswick Convention, THE KESWICK
WEEK, an annual report of the meeting at Keswick.

The well-known motto of the Convention, founded with the aim of "the promotion of practical holiness," is "All One in Christ Jesus."
Doctrinal and ecclesiastical differences are
minimized for one week each year as evangelical Christians gather to pursue a life of
personal holiness. In classical theological
categories, they strive together for sanctification (progressive) attained by a suppression of sinful desires and tendencies within
individual men.

Keswick, albeit often ignored by church historians, has had an influence during the past
century upon the Christian world far out of
proportion to its humble, faltering beginnings. Its followers have sought to trans-
plant the dynamic of the Keswick Convention,
resulting in "Keswick" camps and conferences
in Canada, India, the United States of America, South Africa, Scotland, Germany, France,
the West Indies, and the Orient. Keswick has
had monumental influence on American Fundamentalism, Pentecostalism, and the American
Holiness Movement.

The method of this essay will be to introduce
the reader to the bibliography of the Keswick
Convention and to indicate sources necessary
for understanding the impact of the Convention around the world. Literature will be
presented around the foci of: (1) History
of Keswick and Its Influence; (2) Resources
for Bibliography; (3) Theological and Biblical Studies; (4) Devotional Literature; (5)
Hymnody; (6) Periodicals; and (7) Historical
Collections. Due to the absence of the usual
denominational or traditional structures, the
history of the Keswick Convention and of its
influence throughout Christendom is the story
of the efforts of and direction given by in-
dividuals within the common cause of the higher life. Therefore, a significant portion of
the data provided herein focuses upon the
lives of illustrious men and women.

HISTORY AND INFLUENCE OF KESWICK

Setting the Stage

In order that a more adequate designation and
understanding of this group can occur, a
sketch of the milieus of the origins of the
movement is offered.

The church in England in the middle of the
nineteenth century was plagued with faltering
popular enthusiasm for the religious institutions, accentuated by the rivalry of three
major religious parties. The High Church
party had been recently invigorated by litur-
gical renewal at the impetus of the Oxford
Movement.[1] The Broad Church party sought to

---

1. The Oxford Movement stimulated an immense
    literature. Especially helpful in under-
standing the movement and its impact are H. P.
Liddon, THE LIFE OF E. B. PUSEY, 4 vols. (London; New York: Longmans, Green, 1893-97);R.W.

revitalize itself on a platform of social
reform and by adopting German theological con-
structs and Darwinian concepts.[2] The Low
Church party[3] was strongly influenced by
British Methodism, emphasizing the Bible and
personal religious experience. Each party
strove to improve the church and to influence
the church politically in favor of its alternative: all of this under the aegis of Anglicanism.[4] Outside Anglicanism, the Plymouth
Brethren and, to some extent, British Methodism offered the alternative of a strict lit-

---

Church, THE OXFORD MOVEMENT. TWELVE YEARS,
1833-1845 (London: Macmillan, 1891); S. Baring-Gould, THE CHURCH REVIVAL (London: Me-
thuen, 1914); S. L. Ollard, A SHORT HISTORY
OF THE OXFORD MOVEMENT (London: A. R. Mow-
bray, 1915). For additional bibliography see
F. L. Cross, ed., OXFORD DICTIONARY OF THE
CHRISTIAN CHURCH, pp. 1001-1002; James Hast-
ings, ed., ENCYCLOPAEDIA OF RELIGION AND ETH-
ICS, IX, (1917), 585-589.

2. For tendencies of this movement, ESSAYS
AND REVIEWS (10th ed.; London: Longman,
Green, Longman, & Roberts, 1862); also F. W.
Cornish, THE ENGLISH CHURCH IN THE NINETEENTH
CENTURY, 2 vols. (London: Macmillan, 1910).
For additional study suggestions see OXFORD
DICTIONARY OF THE CHRISTIAN CHURCH, p. 199.

3. The Low Church party was commonly termed
"Evangelical." See J. H. Overton, THE
EVANGELICAL REVIVAL IN THE EIGHTEENTH CENTURY
(London: Longmans, Green, 1900), and H. G. C.
Moule, THE EVANGELICAL SCHOOL IN THE CHURCH
OF ENGLAND (London: J. Nisbet, 1901).

4. The biographical study of the proponents
of the various options in the Church of
England is of primary interest.

eralistic interpretation of Scripture, a conservative pietistic lifestyle, and a simple faith. But it was the Low Church party and other "evangelicals" from within the Anglican tradition that were to provide the majority of the Keswickians.

A second important factor in the origins of the Keswick Movement was the concern for the higher life, resulting from the overflow of American pietistic revivalism;[5] or, as phrased by Robert S. Fletcher, HISTORY OF OBERLIN COLLEGE (Oberlin: Oberlin College, 1943), "the Oberlinizing of England."[6]   Asa

---

5.   Although the most immediate stimuli came from America, Keswick apologists trace their heritage in earlier writers. W. H. Griffith Thomas observes in an essay, "The Literature of Keswick," in C. F. Harford's THE KESWICK CONVENTION, ITS MESSAGE, ITS METHOD AND ITS MEN (London: Marshall Brothers, n.d.), p. 223, "... the roots of the distinctive teachings can easily be traced in the writings of Walter Marshall, William Law, John Wesley, Fletcher of Madeley, Thomas á Kempis, Brother Lawrence, Madame Guyon, the letters of Samuel Rutherford and the Memoir of McCheyne." Of Walter Marshall, THE GOSPEL MYSTERY OF SANCTIFICATION (1692), Thomas comments, p. 223, "...[in Marshall], the essential theology of the KESWICK MOVEMENT is clearly seen;..." The Bonars and George Müller were also influential. See also M. E. Dieter, "The Holiness Revival in Nineteenth Century Europe," WESLEYAN THEOLOGICAL JOURNAL 9, (1974), 15-27. See also Dieter, "Revivalism and Holiness," Ph.D. dissertation at Temple University,1973, available in bound copy from University Microfilms, Ann Arbor, Michigan, order number 73-18, 681.

6.   Also see the chronicle by a former President of Oberlin College, James H. Fair-

Mahan[7] and Charles Grandison Finney[8] visited
England in 1849 and met with significant successes in evangelistic work, building upon
the impact of their writings, especially Finney's LECTURES ON REVIVALS OF RELIGION (New

---

child, OBERLIN: THE COLONY AND THE COLLEGE
1833-1883 (Oberlin: E. J. Goodrich, 1883).

7. Asa Mahan, like Upham, has been appropri-
    ated by the Holiness, Pentecostal, and
Keswick Movements. See note 15 in Donald W.
Dayton, THE AMERICAN HOLINESS MOVEMENT, A BIB-
LIOGRAPHIC INTRODUCTION. Mr. Dayton in 1973
read papers at both the Wesleyan Theological
Society and the Society of Pentecostal Studies which should soon be available in the or-
gans of the respective societies. Barbara
Zikmund's Duke University Ph.D. dissertation,
"Asa Mahan and Oberlin Perfectionism," available through University Microfilms in hard-
bound copy (University Microfilms order #70-
11, 599), is a good introduction both to the
genius of Mahan and to literature by and
about him.

Mahan's philosophical writings continue to at-
tract attention, especially, A SYSTEM OF IN-
TELLECTUAL PHILOSOPHY (New York: Saxon & Miles,
1845), A CRITICAL HISTORY OF PHILOSOPHY, 2
vols. (New York: Phillips and Hunt, 1883),
and SCIENCE OF MORAL PHILOSOPHY (Oberlin:
Fitch, 1848).

8. Charles Grandison Finney's most signifi-
    cant volume, LECTURES ON REVIVALS OF RELI-
GION, ed. William G. McLoughlin (Cambridge·
Harvard University Press, 1960), (original
ed. 1835). His MEMOIRS OF CHARLES G. FIN-
NEY (New York: Revell, 1876), have been kept
in print by Revell as THE AUTOBIOGRAPHY OF
CHARLES G. FINNEY. See also Aaron Merritt
Hills, LIFE OF CHARLES G. FINNEY (Cincinnati:
Office of GOD'S REVIVALIST, 1902).

York: Leavitt and Lord, 1835) and Mahan's
SCRIPTURE DOCTRINE OF CHRISTIAN PERFECTION;
WITH OTHER KINDRED SUBJECTS ILLUSTRATED AND
CONFIRMED IN A SERIES OF DISCOURSES DESIGNED
TO THROW LIGHT ON THE WAY OF HOLINESS (Boston:
D. S. King, 1839).   Mahan had also received
attention in philosophical circles (see note
7).   The Scottish realistic philosophy pio-
neered by Thomas Reid, culminating in the
work of Sir William Hamilton under whom C. G.
Moore and his father studied, provided a foundation which Mahan's perfectionism and Finney's revivalism interpenetrated to undergird
a significant social reform movement.   The result of primary interest for this essay is
the influence of the men and their writings
on others who would sensitize the conscious-
ness of the British churches regarding personal holiness; for example, I. E. Page and
John Brash, co-editors of THE KING'S HIGHWAY,
Thornley Smith, Charles Grandison Moore who
edited DIVINE LIFE (British Wesleyan-Holiness),
also LIFE OF FAITH during the later tenure of
Evan Hopkins.   Moore, named after Finney, was
a close friend of Mahan and later editor of
his works and executor of his estate.   He
continuously added an "Oberlin" perspective
to the Keswickian and Methodist-Holiness periodicals which he edited.

Also influential was the indefatigable James
Caughey.[9]   Caughey, who had been closely, as-
sociated with Phoebe Palmer and influenced by
Mahan and Finney, began revivalistic tours in

---

9.   In addition to the works cited, HELPS TO
     A LIFE OF HOLINESS AND USEFULNESS; OR,
REVIVAL MISCELLANIES, eds. Ralph W. Allen and
Daniel Wise (Boston: J.P. Magee, 1851), and
SHOWERS OF BLESSING FROM CLOUDS OF MERCY; selected from the Journal and other writings of
the Rev. James Caughey (Boston: J. P. Magee,
1857).

England as early as 1841. His successes are chronicled in THE TRIUMPH OF TRUTH AND CONTINENTAL LETTERS AND SKETCHES FROM THE JOURNAL, LETTERS AND SERMONS OF THE REV. JAMES CAUGHEY WITH AN INTRODUCTION BY JOSEPH CASTLE (Philadelphia: Higgins and Perkinpine, 1857), and EARNEST CHRISTIANITY, ILLUSTRATED; OR, SELECTIONS FROM THE JOURNAL OF REV. JAMES CAUGHEY WITH A BRIEF SKETCH OF MR. CAUGHEY'S LIFE by Daniel Wise (Boston: J. P. Magee, 1855).

In addition to the ministry and writings of these men, the writings of Thomas Upham[10] and William Arthur[11] were widely circulated.

The revival of 1857-1858 has been described by Timothy Smith, REVIVALISM AND SOCIAL REFORM (New York: Abingdon, 1957),and by J. Edwin Orr, THE SECOND EVANGELICAL AWAKENING IN BRITAIN (London & Edinburgh: Marshall,

---

10. Thomas Upham influenced both the Holiness Movement in America and Keswick. His LIFE AND RELIGIOUS OPINIONS AND EXPERIENCES OF MADAME DE LA MOTHE GUYON (N.Y.: Harper, 1847), has been frequently reprinted by H. R. Allenson as LIFE OF MADAME GUYON. PRINCIPLES OF THE INTERIOR OR HIDDEN LIFE (Boston: D. S. King, 1843), and other works are analyzed by Gregory Peck, "Dr. Upham's Works," METHODIST QUARTERLY REVIEW 28 (1846), 248-265. See also B. B. Warfield, PERFECTIONISM, II (New York: Oxford University Press, 1931), 337-459, and Melvin Easterday Dieter, "Revivalism and Holiness," chapter 2, pp. 64-68 and notes, 153-164.

11. British Wesleyan-Methodist William Arthur, TONGUE OF FIRE (London: Hamilton, Adams, 1856),was widely circulated in American Holiness, Pentecostal and British Keswick circles; its continued influence is attested by frequent reprintings.

Morgan and Scott, 1949), and THE SECOND EVAN-
GELICAL AWAKENING IN AMERICA (London: Mar-
shall, Morgan & Scott, 1952). Both of Orr's
books were abridged into a more popular ac-
count, THE SECOND EVANGELICAL AWAKENING, AN
ACCOUNT OF THE SECOND WORLDWIDE EVANGELICAL
REVIVAL BEGINNING IN THE MID NINETEENTH CEN-
TURY (London & Edinburgh: Marshall, Morgan
and Scott, 1955). A portion of the first vol-
ume was printed under the title, AMERICA'S
GREAT REVIVAL (Elizabethtown, Pa.: McBeth
Press, 1957). More accessible is his THE
LIGHT OF THE NATIONS: EVANGELICAL RENEWAL
AND ADVANCE IN THE NINETEENTH CENTURY (Grand
Rapids: Eerdmans, 1965), which is a more gen-
eral discussion of the period.

The message of the American-originated revival was then transported abroad. Mahan re-
turned to England, where he was in continual
demand as a speaker; James Caughey worked in
close cooperation with Phoebe and Dr. W. C.
Palmer whose efforts are detailed in FOUR
YEARS IN THE OLD WORLD; COMPRISING THE TRA-
VELS, INCIDENTS AND EVANGELISTIC LABORS OF
DR. AND MRS. PALMER IN ENGLAND, IRELAND, SCOT-
LAND AND WALES (New York: Foster and Palmer,
1866). Finney undertook another tour of the
British Isles. The dramatic results have
been ably chronicled by Orr.

During the two decades following the English
revivals of 1858-1859 holiness conventions
were going on all over England. Mahan,
through his involvement in the pre-Keswick
conferences discussed below and his editorship of DIVINE LIFE, helped to unify the higher life aspirations arising from the "Oberlinizing of England" and to focus them in the
direction of the Wesleyan-Holiness theological
heritage combined with an emphasis on the baptism of the Holy Spirit. Thus, the ground-
work was laid for the visits of the Moody-
Sankey team, the Robert Pearsall Smiths and
William Edwin Boardman to England, France

and Germany.[12]

---

12.   William Edwin Boardman, a product of the
      "Burned-Over District" of New York and
a graduate of Lane Theological Seminary, Cincinnati, was a controversial promoter of the
higher life. Closely related to the American
Holiness Movement, his very influential book,
THE HIGHER CHRISTIAN LIFE (Boston: Henry
Hoyt, 1859, revised 1871), argued that every
Christian must achieve a higher plane of
Christian life, entered by an act of faith as
at justification. His theological perspective is critiqued by Jacob J. Abbott, "Boardman's Higher Christian Life," BIBLIOTHECA
SACRA AND BIBLICAL REPOSITORY, 17 (July 1860),
508-535; by John A. Todd, "Law of Spiritual
Growth," THE BIBLICAL REPERTORY AND PRINCE-
TON REVIEW, 32 (1860), 608-640. Both of
these reviewers take Boardman to task for
faulty scholarship and theological error.
Boardman's work is also evaluated by Warfield, PERFECTIONISM, II, 463-494. The most
severe critique is that of Henry A. Boardman,
"THE HIGHER LIFE" DOCTRINE OF SANCTIFICATION
TRIED BY THE WORD OF GOD (Philadelphia: Presbyterian Board of Publication, 1877), which
serves to evaluate the entire resultant movement. A less influential work was IN THE POW-
ER OF THE SPIRIT; OR, CHRISTIAN EXPERIENCE IN
THE LIGHT OF THE BIBLE (London: Daldy, Isbister, 1875). Despite the obvious shortcomings
of his work, Boardman, perhaps more than any-
one else, raised interest in the possibility
of the higher Christian life. His life has
been chronicled by his wife, THE LIFE AND LA-
BORS OF THE REV. W. E. BOARDMAN (New York:
Appleton, 1887). It is enthusiastic and at
times self-contradictory but no more adequate
work has been produced.

W. E. Boardman, THE HIGHER CHRISTIAN LIFE
(Boston: Henry Hoyt, 1858), is credited by

In 1872 Mr. & Mrs. Robert Pearsall Smith,[13] Quakers from the American Holiness Movement, sought respite in England from their American religious and mercantile labors. They

---

Steven Barabas, SO GREAT SALVATION, THE HISTORY AND MESSAGE OF THE KESWICK MOVEMENT (Westwood, N. J.: Revell, 1952), p. 16, as being the most influential in arousing interest in sanctification and the Spirit-filled life.

In addition to Mahan, Boardman, and Arthur, the writings of Richard Poole, CENTER AND CIRCLE OF EVANGELICAL RELIGION; OR, PERFECT LIFE (London: Jarrold, 1873),and Hannah Whitall Smith, THE CHRISTIAN'S SECRET OF A HAPPY LIFE (New York: Revell, 1875),had wide and influential circulation; as did the writings of George Müller,NARRATIVE OF THE LORD'S DEALINGS WITH GEORGE MÜLLER, (London: Nisbet, 1895),1st ed., 1837 and in later American editions, THE LIFE OF TRUST: with an introduction by Francis Wayland. THE DIARY OF GEORGE MÜLLER, (London: Pickering & Inglis, 1954),was edited by A. Rendle Short. There are biographies by W. H. Harding, THE LIFE OF GEORGE MÜLLER, A RECORD OF FAITH TRIUMPHANT (London: Morgan & Scott, 1914), Basil W. Miller, GEORGE MÜLLER, THE MAN OF FAITH; A BIOGRAPHY OF ONE OF THE GREATEST PRAYER-WARRIORS OF THE PAST CENTURY (Grand Rapids: Zondervan, 1951), and the often reprinted work of A. T. Pierson, GEORGE MÜLLER OF BRISTOL AND HIS WITNESS TO A PRAYER-HEARING GOD (New York: Baker and Taylor, 1899), containing a preface by Müller's son-in-law, James Wright.

13. Robert Pearsall Smith has not been the subject of any extensive critical biography. Some details may be gleaned from the writings of his wife, Hannah Whitall Smith, and their son, Logan Pearsall Smith,

were soon involved in meetings of select
groups in private homes, and in 1873, togeth-

---

but most of his life remains shrouded from
view. Most helpful are Logan Pearsall Smith,
UNFORGOTTEN YEARS (Boston: Little, Brown,
1939); Hannah Whitall Smith; THE RECORD OF A
HAPPY LIFE: BEING MEMORIALS OF FRANKLIN WHIT-
ALL SMITH (Philadelphia, Privately printed,
1873); "Smith, Robert Pearsall," DIE RELIGION
IN GESCHICHTE UND GEGENWART, VI 1962 (3rd ed.;
Tübingen: Mohr),112; "The Religious Experience of R. Pearsall Smith," THE CHRISTIAN OB-
SERVER 75 (1875, London), 830 ff., 926 ff.;
76 (1876), 60 ff. Also available but less
biographical are Fr. Winkler, "Robert Pear-
sall Smith und der Perfectionismus" in Fried-
rich D. Kropatscheck, BIBLISCHE ZEIT UND
STREITFRAGEN ZUR AUFKLÄRUNG DER GEBILDETEN
Series 10 (Berlin-Lichterfielde: Edwin Runge,
1914), 410-422 and Johannes Jüngst, AMERI-
KANISCHER METHODISMUS IN DEUTSCHLAND UND RO-
BERT PEARSALL SMITH (Gotha, F. A. Perthes,
1875). See also B. B. Warfield, PERFECTION-
ISM, II (New York: Oxford University Press,
1931) ,and M. E. Dieter, "Revivalism and Holiness." The Cowper-Temple Correspondence,
Broadlands Archives has material relating primarily to the period of the Broadlands Conference.

His own writings were very influential in pro-
voking interest in the higher life in England.
HOLINESS THROUGH FAITH; LIGHT ON THE WAY OF
HOLINESS (London: Morgan and Scott, 1870),
"WALK IN THE LIGHT." WORDS OF COUNSEL TO
THOSE WHO HAVE ENTERED INTO "THE REST OF
FAITH" (London: n.p.,1873), had a lasting in-
fluence. As editor of THE CHRISTIAN'S PATH-
WAY TO POWER he influenced the revival move-
ments of America and England. An extensive
listing of Smith's writings is found in War-
field, PERFECTIONISM, II, 510.

er with W. E. Boardman they held a series of
breakfasts focusing on the subject of the
higher life. This served as a prelude to
three conferences or conventions which, in
turn, spawned the Keswick Convention.

The support of W. Cowper-Temple (later Lord
Mount Temple),made possible the Conference
of July 17-23, 1874 on his Broadlands estate.[14]
One hundred attended, including George Macdonald, Theodore Monod,[15] Mrs. Amanda Smith,[16]

---

14. Material relevant to the Broadlands Con-
     vention may be found in the Cowper-Tem-
ple Correspondence at the Broadlands Archives;
in Edna Jackson, THE LIFE THAT IS LIFE INDEED:
REMEMBRANCES OF THE BROADLANDS CONFERENCES
(London: Nisbet, 1910), and in most histories of the KESWICK MOVEMENT.

15. Theodore Monod, a pastor in Paris, influ-
     enced by Robert Pearsall Smith, was a
well known figure in British higher life meetings. His books and tracts are still being
reprinted, primarily by "Back to the Bible
Broadcast," Box 82808, Lincoln, Nebraska 68501.
LOOKING UNTO JESUS (Lincoln: BBB, 1973), 22
pps., contains a note indicating 625,000 copies of this tract have been published. THE
GIFT OF LIFE (London: Morgan & Scott, 1912),
THE GIFT OF GOD (London: Morgan & Scott,
1876), and DENYING SELF, ed. H. F. Bowker
(London: Frome, 1878), and LIFE MORE ABUN-
DANT (London: Morgan & Scott, 1881),are
all books of addresses delivered at higher
life conferences, primarily at Keswick. No
biographical material has been found, nor is
there a comprehensive list of Monod's works.
He was the author of the famous Keswick song,
"None of Self and All of Thee."

16. Mrs. Amanda Smith, a former slave with
     little formal education, traveled through-

the Black holiness evangelist, and Canon Wilberforce. Robert Pearsall Smith was the chairman. Out of the concern that this type of conference be more widely available, the Oxford Convention,[17] August 29-September 7, 1874, featured Robert Pearsall Smith as chairman and principal speaker. His wife, Hannah Whitall Smith,[18] Theodore Monod, Evan H.

---

out the world "representing" the American Holiness Movement. Her AUTOBIOGRAPHY; THE STORY OF THE LORD'S DEALING WITH MRS. AMANDA SMITH, THE COLORED EVANGELIST, was published in 1893 by Meyer & Bro. of Chicago and recently reprinted (Noblesville, Ind.: J. Edwin Newby, 1962). See also, M. H. Cadbury, THE LIFE OF AMANDA SMITH, "THE AFRICAN SYBIL, THE CHRISTIAN SAINT," with an introduction by J. Rendel Harris (Birmingham, England: Cornish Bros., 1916), and Marshall William Taylor, THE LIFE, TRAVELS, LABORS, AND HELPERS OF MRS. AMANDA SMITH, THE FAMOUS NEGRO MISSIONARY EVANGELIST (Cincinnati: Cranston and Stowe, 1886).

17. ACCOUNT OF THE UNION MEETING FOR THE PROMOTION OF SCRIPTURAL HOLINESS, HELD AT OXFORD, August 29th to September 7th, 1874 (Chicago: Revell, 1874), is a rather wordy but detailed account of the proceedings. See also ADVOCATE OF CHRISTIAN HOLINESS 5 (1874), 134-135 and THE METHODIST MAGAZINE 17 (1874), 992-997. These and other Holiness Movement and/or Methodist periodicals carried enthusiastic reports of the convention.

18. Hannah Whitall Smith, as with her husband Robert Pearsall Smith, (see above) has not been the subject of critical biographies. She gives an account of their early religious experiences in THE RECORD OF A HAPPY LIFE: BEING MEMORIALS OF FRANKLIN WHITALL SMITH (Philadelphia: Lippincott, 1873), and of her own pilgrimage in THE UN-

Hopkins,[19] Asa Mahan, and W. E. Boardman also
spoke.

SELFISHNESS OF GOD, AND HOW I DISCOVERED IT
(London: J. Nisbet, 1903); the American edi-
tion, THE UNSELFISHNESS OF GOD, AND HOW I DIS-
COVERED IT; A SPIRITUAL AUTOBIOGRAPHY (N.Y.:
Revell, 1903).

Her granddaughter, Ray Strachey (Rachel Cos-
telloe), A QUAKER GRANDMOTHER (N.Y.: Revell,
1914), chronicles her last years, and in RELI-
GIOUS FANATICISM; EXTRACTS FROM THE PAPERS OF
HANNAH WHITALL SMITH (London: Faber & Gwyer,
1928),presents aspects of her religious experiences. Logan Pearsall Smith, her son, published his reminiscences in UNFORGOTTEN YEARS
(Boston: Little, Brown, 1939),and her letters
in A RELIGIOUS REBEL: THE LETTERS OF "H.W.S."
(London: Nisbet, 1949),with a biographical
preface by Robert Gathorne-Hardy.[American edition: PHILADELPHIA QUAKER; THE LETTERS OF HAN-
NAH WHITALL SMITH (N.Y.: Harcourt,Brace,1950]).

Mrs. Smith was a very influential writer, far
surpassing her husband. THE CHRISTIAN'S SE-
CRET OF A HAPPY LIFE (N.Y.: Revell, 1875),orig-
inally published in her husband's periodical THE CHRISTIAN'S PATHWAY TO POWER, has been
continuously reprinted and translated. Also
important are: BIBLE READINGS ON THE PROGRES-
SIVE DEVELOPMENT OF TRUTH AND EXPERIENCE IN
THE O.T. SCRIPTURES (London: Elliot Stock,
1878), BIBLE STUDIES ON THE HIGHER LIFE (London: Longley, 1891), THE VEIL UPLIFTED; OR,
THE BIBLE ITS OWN INTERPRETER (London: Longley, 1886), LIVING IN THE SUNSHINE (N.Y.: Revell, 1906), published also as THE GOD OF ALL
COMFORT (London: Nisbet, 1906), THE INTERIOR
LIFE (London: Longley, 1886), and EVERY-DAY
RELIGION; OR, THE COMMON-SENSE TEACHING OF
THE BIBLE (N.Y.: Revell, 1893).

19. Evan Henry Hopkins (1837-1918), for many
     years the leader of Keswick and the chief

22

The Brighton Convention,[20] May 29-June 7,
1875, again with Smith as chairman, featured
speakers of later Keswick fame: E. H. Hopkins, Stevenson A. Blackwood, H. W. Webb-Peploe and Theodore Monod. An exciting success,
cheered on by Moody, it was the Smiths' last
convention in England. The stage was set for
the Keswick Convention.

---

guide in matters of doctrine, is the subject
of a study by his friend, Alexander Smellie,
EVAN HENRY HOPKINS. A MEMOIR (London: Mar-
shall Bros., 1920), and in an introductory
appreciation by Fred Mitchell in a reprint of
Hopkins' most influential book, THE LAW OF
LIBERTY IN THE SPIRITUAL LIFE (Philadelphia:
The Sunday School Times, 1952). The first
edition was published in London in 1884 by
Marshall Brothers. Other significant works
by Hopkins are BROKEN BREAD FOR DAILY USE,
BEING THOUGHTS AND COMMENTS ON THE HEADLINE
TEXTS OF "DAILY LIGHT ON THE DAILY PATH" (Lon-
don: Samuel Bagster, 1895), HIDDEN YET POS-
SESSED (London: Marshall Bros., 1894), TALKS
WITH BEGINNERS IN THE DIVINE LIFE (London:
Marshall Bros., 1909), THOUGHTS ON LIFE AND
GODLINESS (London: Hodder & Stoughton, 1878),
and THE WALK THAT PLEASES GOD (London: Mar-
shall Bros., 1887).

20. RECORD OF THE CONVENTION FOR THE PROMO-
     TION OF SCRIPTURAL HOLINESS HELD AT
BRIGHTON, May 29th to June 7th, 1875 (Brighton:
W. J. Smith, 1875), is a detailed account of
the meetings, messages, and responses. Near-
ly eight thousand people attended the Convention including participants from France and
Germany. The emphasis as recorded, is on the
internal experience; little social concern is
reflected, which a few decades before had
been the heart cry of the American Holiness
Movement which provided the impetus for Brighton. Indicative is the favorite hymn of the

Histories of Keswick

The Reverend T. D. H. Battersby,[21] who attended the Oxford Convention, and a friend, Robert Wilson, initiated the first Keswick Convention and scheduled it to begin three weeks after the Brighton Convention. It was to be chaired by Smith, but he cancelled due to reasons still obscure, leaving Battersby supported by speakers Webb-Peploe, George R. Thornton, T. Phillips, H. F. Bowker, T. M. Croome and Murray Shipley to lead the circa 400 in

Convention, "Jesus Saves Me Now." Brighton was middle class in expression and in values. The entire movement therefore tended to be more "quietistic" than the American Holiness Movement. This is true, relatively, even today.

21. Canon Thomas Dundas Harford Battersby may be called the founder of the Keswick Convention. An Oxford graduate who had gone from High Church to Broad Church, he attended Oxford and Brighton, experiencing "resting faith." His sons wrote an apology for his life and beliefs, MEMOIR OF T. D. HARFORD-BATTERSBY, LATE VICAR OF ST. JOHN'S, KESWICK. . .TOGETHER WITH SOME ACCOUNT OF THE KESWICK CONVENTION. With a preface by H. C. G. Moule (London: Seeley, 1890). Battersby wrote and published several sermons on the holy life, CHRIST IN THE HEART (London: Wertheim, 1860), HIGHER ATTAINMENTS IN CHRISTIAN HOLINESS, AND HOW TO PROMOTE THEM (London: Nisbet, 1875). In 1878 he published BONDAGE OR LIBERTY? A SKETCH OF ST. PAUL'S TEACHING IN ROMANS VI-VIII (London: Hodder & Stoughton), a doctrinal apologetic for a Keswickian understanding of original sin, justification and sanctification. Battersby edited REMINISCENCES OF THE KESWICK CONVENTION (London: Partridge, 1879), discussed above.

attendance into the higher Christian life.
The first meeting has been the focal point of
several histories of the movement. Evan Hopkins, "Preliminary Stages" and Webb-Peploe
and E. W. Moore, "Early Keswick Conventions,"
chapters in THE KESWICK CONVENTION, ITS MES-
SAGE, ITS METHOD AND ITS MEN (London: Marshall Bros., 1907),are accounts by participants, as are E. H. Hopkins, THE STORY OF KES-
WICK, Eighteenth Convention, 1892 (London:
Life of Faith, 1892), and THE KESWICK JUBILEE
SOUVENIR, THE STORY OF THE CONVENTION'S FIFTY
YEARS' MINISTRY AND INFLUENCE (London: Marshall Bros., 1925). These are short, popular,
and enthusiastically uncritical. Walter B.
Sloan, THESE SIXTY YEARS, THE STORY OF THE
KESWICK CONVENTION (London: Pickering and Inglis, n.d.,1935?),is a chronicle of the movement. Tedious in laborious detail, it plods
through the years reading rather like minutes
kept for business sessions. There are good
photographs of the most influential men of
the movement, but not a solitary bibliographic clue appears to lead the reader to his
sources. Arthur Tappan Pierson,[22] THE KES-
WICK MOVEMENT, ITS PRECEPT AND PRACTICE,
with introduction by Rev. Evan H. Hopkins
(New York & London: Funk & Wagnalls, 1903)is
an apologetic history of the movement and an
effort to present the movement's theological

---

22. ARTHUR TAPPAN PIERSON, A SPIRITUAL WAR-
     RIOR, MIGHTY IN THE SCRIPTURES; A LEADER
IN THE MODERN MISSIONARY CRUSADE (New York:
Revell, 1912), is by his son, Delavan Leonard
Pierson. An able apologist for the Keswick
distinctives, A. T. P. wrote THE KESWICK MOVE-
MENT IN PRECEPT AND PRACTICE (New York: Funk
& Wagnalls, 1903), and FORWARD MOVEMENTS OF
THE LAST HALF CENTURY (New York: Funk & Wag-
nalls, 1900). Many of his works are listed
in Jones, A GUIDE TO THE STUDY OF THE HOLI-
NESS MOVEMENT.

foci. It is written carefully in popular style.

Battersby, REMINISCENCES OF THE KESWICK CON-
VENTION, 1879, WITH ADDRESSES BY PASTOR OTTO
STOCKMAYER (London: S. W. Partridge, 1879),
is a valuable bit of data (40 pp.). Of primary importance but hard to find and conse-
quently ignored is Battersby, MEMOIR OF T. D.
HARFORD BATTERSBY TOGETHER WITH SOME ACCOUNTS
OF THE KESWICK CONVENTION, by two of his sons
with a preface by H. C. G. Moule (London:
Seeley, 1890). Evan H. Hopkins, that grand
patriarch of the first decades, left his memoirs, A STANDARD BEARER OF FAITH AND HOLINESS;
REMINISCENCES WITH A MEMOIR BY THE AUTHOR
(London: Morgan and Scott, 1919). It is of
little scientific value but its 47 pages provide one view of the beginnings.

From this same era comes J.B. Figgis, KESWICK
FROM WITHIN (London: Marshall Bros., 1914),
an indispensable but less than fluid commentary on the conventions. Figgis is an apologist for the movement as is the American professor at Crozer Theological Seminary, E. H.
Johnson, THE HIGHEST LIFE, A STORY OF SHORT-
COMINGS AND A GOAL; INCLUDING A FRIENDLY ANAL-
YSIS OF THE KESWICK MOVEMENT (New York: A. C.
Armstrong, 1901),which is not as friendly as
the title would lead one to suspect. The British version of Keswick is given a higher rating than are the modifications of Moody at
Northfield.

Steven Barabas, SO GREAT SALVATION, THE HIS-
TORY AND MESSAGE OF THE KESWICK CONVENTION
(Westwood, N. J.: Revell, 1952; London: Marshall, Morgan & Scott, 1952),with a preface
by Fred Mitchell, Chairman of the Keswick Convention Council 1948-1951, is still the standard history of the movement. It contains a
sketch of the beginnings of the convention,
an exposition of Keswickian teaching, biographical sketches of some Keswick leaders

and the most extensive bibliography of material related to Keswick and to the men of the
movement. J. C. Pollock, THE KESWICK STORY,
THE AUTHORIZED HISTORY OF THE KESWICK CONVEN-
TION (London: Hodder & Stoughton, 1964), is
an attempt to popularize the history of the
movement. The result is much more concern
with dramatic effect than with the facts. It
is of little scholarly value having neither
documentation, bibliography nor concern for
critical historical methodology. It is, however, the only chronicle of the World War II
era and after, when Keswick was preoccupied
with theology rather than history (see below,
Theology and Biblical Studies).

Those outside the Keswick Convention made only limited efforts to analyze and understand
the genius of Keswick. B. B. Warfield, PER-
FECTIONISM, 2 vols. (New York: Oxford University Press, 1931), gives considerable space to
a critique of the early influences on the
movement. He is very critical of their concerns. PERFECTIONISM has been reissued in a
one volume edition (Presbyterian and Reformed,
1958),with the material on Thomas Upham de-
leted. More helpful and without the flaming
prejudice of Warfield is the superb work of
Melvin Easterday Dieter "Revivalism and Holiness" (see above note 5), Temple University
Ph.D. dissertation, 1973, University Microfilms Order Number 73-18, 681. His article,
"From Vineland and Menheim to Brighton and
Berlin: The Holiness Revival in Nineteenth-
Century Europe," WESLEYAN THEOLOGICAL JOURNAL
9 (1974), 15-27, draws heavily upon the dissertation, and is a sober, responsible analysis of the background of Keswick.

Finally, Herbert F. Stevenson, editor of LIFE
OF FAITH has prepared a series of supplements
to that periodical featuring the history of
LIFE OF FAITH, formerly THE CHRISTIAN'S PATH-
WAY TO POWER founded by Robert Pearsall Smith
and later edited by William E. Boardman,

Charles G. Moore[23] and Evan H. Hopkins, and
J. K. Maclean. As the closest, although inde-
pendent, organ of the Keswick Movement, a
study of its history quite naturally shed
light on Keswick.

Influence of Keswick

The Welsh Revival. A fascinating problem of
nationalism and of historiography is the rela-
tionship of the Keswick Convention to the
Welsh Revival. Mrs. Jessie Penn-Lewis, THE
AWAKENING IN WALES AND SOME OF THE HIDDEN
SPRINGS...WITH AN INTRODUCTION TO THE WELSH
REVIVALS BY J. CYNDDYLAN JONES (London: Marshall Bros., 1905), indicates that the roots
of the revival in Wales were to be found in
Keswick. The same approach is taken by Rhyc
Bevan Jones, RENT HEAVENS, THE REVIVAL OF
1904, SOME OF ITS HIDDEN SPRINGS AND PROMI-
NENT RESULTS (London: S. Martin, 1931). However, the assertion of dependency when voiced
by F. B. Meyer provoked a running newspaper
battle and eventual rejection of the Welsh Revival by Keswick.[24] For additional detail

---

23. Charles Grandison Moore was de facto ed-
    itor during the tenure of Evan Hopkins.
It was important to the early leaders that
close ties be maintained with the Anglican
Church, and Moore was a Methodist. He contributed a volume to the Keswick Library, 11,
"THINGS WHICH CANNOT BE SHAKEN" (London: Marshall Bros., 1894), and abridged the autobiography of Amanda Smith for British readers.

24. See A. T. Pierson, "The Revival in Wales,"
    EXPERIENCE, (July-Sept., 1905), pp. 94-97.
He suggests that the revival had its origin
in a "prayer-circle" formed at Keswick, 1902,
consisting of Pierson, Moore, Albert Head and
F. Paynter. The revival was compared to that
of 1859 and heralded as "the beginning of the
latter rain."

and references to articles, see Eifion Evans,
THE WELSH REVIVAL OF 1904 (Port Talbot, Gla-
morgan: Evangelical Movement of Wales, 1969),
the best analysis of the revival. J. C. Pollock, THE KESWICK STORY (London: Hodder &
Stoughton, 1964),gives the Keswick Convention's perspective on the interaction. Accounts by participants and onlookers include
John Vyrnwy Morgan, THE WELSH REVIVAL, 1904-
5, A RETROSPECT AND A CRITICISM (London:
Chapman & Hall, 1909),who takes the phenomenon to task for its lack of tangible results
beyond the rhetoric. David Matthews, I SAW
THE WELSH REVIVAL (Chicago: Moody Press,
1957),is more popular, but helpful. J. Edwin
Orr, THE FLAMING TONGUE, THE IMPACT OF THE
TWENTIETH CENTURY REVIVALS (Chicago: Moody
Press, 1973),seeks to measure the influence
of the Welsh Revival, indicating its significance for understanding the Pentecostal Movement in America. An account of the Welsh Revival by the American Holiness leader, S. B.
Shaw, THE GREAT REVIVAL IN WALES, ALSO AN AC-
COUNT OF THE GREAT REVIVAL IN IRELAND IN 1859
(Chicago: S. B. Shaw, 1906),includes reports
by Mrs. M. Baxter, F. B. Meyers and R. A. Torrey. The book figured prominently in the Azu-
sa Street revivals, being widely read by the
participants.

The life of Evan Roberts, whose meteoric rise
and demise encompassed the greatest portion
of this revival, has been chronicled by D. M.
Phillips, EVAN ROBERTS, THE GREAT WELSH REVIV-
ALIST AND HIS WORD, 3rd ed. (London: Marshall
Bros., 1906). This is a tedious, enthusiastic
reiteration of the bulk of Roberts' revivalistic efforts. A considerable quantity of correspondence is printed here. Mrs. Jessie
Penn-Lewis, who cared for Roberts after his
withdrawal from ministry (due, it is supposed,
to a mental breakdown) became the leader of
the continuing revival movement. In collabo-
ration with Roberts, she wrote WAR ON THE
SAINTS, A TEXTBOOK FOR BELIEVERS ON THE WORK

OF DECEIVING-SPIRITS AMONG THE CHILDREN OF
GOD (London: Marshall Bros., 1912). She
founded the OVERCOMER, a deeper life period-
ical, and served for several years as its ed-
itor. Her memoirs were published by Mary N.
Garrard, MRS. PENN-LEWIS: A MEMOIR, COMPILED
LARGELY FROM MRS. PENN-LEWIS' DIARIES AND
NOTES (London: Overcomer Book Room, 1931).

The German Holiness Movement. Between the
Oxford and Brighton conventions, Robert Pearsall Smith made a well received tour-crusade
through Germany sponsored by the Free Churches. The literature on this tour and its results in German ecclesiastical history is
fragmentary. The best English language summary of the Holiness Revival in Germany is in
Melvin E. Dieter's, "Revivalism and Holiness,"
chapter IV (see note, 5).

The most prolific historian of the German Holiness Movement is Paul Fleisch, whose DIE
HEILIGUNGSBEWEGUNG VON WESLEY BIS BOARDMAN,
VOL. 1 of ZUR GESCHICHTE DER HEILIGUNGSBEWEG-
UNG, Erstes Heft (Leipzig: H. G. Wallman,
1910), must be the starting point of any future study. Emphasizing Boardman, he also
discusses Oberlin theology as represented by
Finney and Mahan. The theology of Thomas Upham and R. P. Smith are also treated. Two of
his articles, "Der Heiligungslehre der Ox-
forder Bewegung" NEUE KIRCHLICHE ZEITSCHRIFT
35 (1924), 49-87 and "Die Entstehung der
deutschen Heiligungsbewegung vor 50 Jahren,"
NEUE KIRCHLICHE ZEITSCHRIFT 38 (1927), 663-
702 trace the influence of Smith, and the
Brighton and Oxford meetings. Fleisch's articles in DIE RELIGION IN GESCHICHTE UND
GEGENWART, 2nd ed., on Mahan, Finney, Smith
and various other holiness leaders and themes
are significant.

Smith's efforts are summarized in Fr. Winkler,
"Robert Pearsall Smith und der Perfectionis-
mus," BIBLISCHE ZEIT- UND STREITFRAGEN ZUR
AUFKLARUNG DES GEBILDETEN 9 (1914), 401-422

and by B. B. Warfield, PERFECTIONISM, II,
503 ff. On German Methodism, see H. Branden-
burg, "Heiligungsbewegung," DIE RELIGION IN
GESCHICHTE UND GEGENWART, III (3rd ed.; Tü-
bingen: Mohr, 1959), 182, Paul F. Douglass,
THE STORY OF GERMAN METHODISM: BIOGRAPHY OF
AN IMMIGRANT SOUL (New York: Methodist Book
Concern, 1939), and A. L. Drummond, GERMAN
PROTESTANTISM SINCE LUTHER (London: Epworth
Pr., 1951).

The movement in Germany which resulted from
the holiness revival has been chronicled by
A. L. Drummond, H. Brandenburg, and Paul F.
Douglass as well as L. Tiesmayer, "Was jeder-
man von der christlichen Gemeinschaftsbewe-
gung in Deutschland wissen muss," DIE RELI-
GION IN GESCHICHTE UND GEGENWART, II (2nd ed.;
Tübingen: Mohr, 1928), 1751-1752, which in-
cludes significant bibliography. Adbel R.
Wentz, GERMANY'S MODERN PIETISTIC MOVEMENT
(n.p.: n.n., n.d.),is excellent as is P.
Fleisch, DIE MODERNE GEMEINSCHAFTBEWEGUNG
IN DEUTSCHLAND: EIN VERSUCH, DIESELBE NACH
IHREN URSPRUENGEN DARZUSTELLEN UND ZU WÜR-
DIGEN (Leipzig: H. G. Wallman, 1903).

Theodor Jellinghaus, Otto Stockmayer and Heinrich Rappard were the most influential theo-
logians of the movement. They and others are
featured in Ernst Modersohn, MEN OF REVIVAL
IN GERMANY (Frankfort am Main: Harold Pub.,
n.d.), a popular exposition of the lives of
these men. Otto Stockmayer was often on the
platform at Keswick, and his SANCTIFIED ONES
(New York: n.n., 1904?), had at least two e-
ditions. Important in Switzerland and Germany
were DIE GNADE IST ERSCHIENEN (München: Ank-
er, 1949), ABRAHAM, DER VATER DER GLÄUBIGEN
(Basel: Brunnen, 1943), and DIE GABE DES
HEILIGEN GEISTES (Basel: n.n., 1898). See
also J. C. Pollock, THE KESWICK STORY, passim,
and DIE RELIGION IN GESCHICHTE UND GEGENWART,
VI (3rd ed.; Tübingen: Mohr, 1962), 386, regarding Stockmayer's life and influence. Sev-

eral of Stockmayer's addresses were edited
by T. D. H. Battersby, REMINISCENCES OF THE
KESWICK CONVENTION, ADDRESSES OF PASTOR STOCK-
MAYER AT THE KESWICK CONVENTION (London: S.
W. Partridge, 1879),and in Stockmayer's, THE
BODY OF CHRIST AND ITS DIVINE ARCHITECT (Lon-
don: J. Snow, 1899).

Theodor Jellinghaus, though less well known
in England and America, was a missionary, pastor, theologian, and biblical expositor, DER
BRIEF PAULI AN DIE RÖMER (Auslegung des Neuen
Testaments, 6, Berlin: Thormann & Goetsch,
1903). His DAS VÖLLIGE, GEGENWÄRTIGE HEIL
DURCH CHRISTUM (Berlin: Prochnow, 1880; 4th
ed. Basel: Kober, Spittlers, 1898), outlined
a rather "Keswickian" understanding of holiness, avoiding the "perfectionist" persuasion
of American Methodism. PHILADELPHIA, a periodical published by the Committee for the Cul-
tivation of Christian Fellowship and Evangelical Piety, was edited with considerable success by Jellinghaus and served as a cohesive
element for the rapidly growing movement.

Foreign Missions. The Keswick Convention has
been an influential force in Christian missions, not so much in terms of direct personal support as in the inspiring of persons to
enter foreign missionary service and in moti-
vating the wealthier churchmen of Britain to
promote and provide for missions. For material relating to this concern see John Pollock,
"Keswick Convention," in CONCISE DICTIONARY
OF THE CHRISTIAN WORLD MISSION, ed. Stephen
Neill (Nashville: Abingdon, 1971), p. 322.
More helpful is the well-indexed HISTORY OF
THE CHURCH MISSIONARY SOCIETY: ITS ENVIRON-
MENT, ITS MEN AND ITS WORK, by Eugene Stock,
Vol. III (London: Church Missionary Society,
1899). This volume is a gold mine of data regarding the development of missionary concern
within the Convention leading to the"Mission-
ary Meetings," under the leadership of Regi-
nald Radcliffe, and to the eventual sending

of Convention missionaries. The first of
these was Amy Carmichael, whose story has
been told by Frank Houghton, AMY CARMICHAEL
OF DOHNAVUR: THE STORY OF A LOVER AND HER
BELOVED (London: S.P.C.K., 1953).

James Hudson Taylor was a key figure in Keswick missions. The China Inland Mission,
which he founded, had many contacts with the
Convention and drew support from it. Taylor's
principal biographers were his son and daughter-in-law, Dr. and Mrs. (Frederick) Howard
Taylor. J. HUDSON TAYLOR, FOUNDER OF THE CHI-
NA INLAND MISSION (Chicago: Moody, 1965),
was abridged by Phyllis Thompson from the
earlier two volume life, HUDSON TAYLOR IN
EARLY YEARS: THE GROWTH OF A SOUL and HUDSON
TAYLOR AND THE CHINA INLAND MISSION: THE
GROWTH OF A WORK OF GOD (London: Morgan &
Scott, 1911-1918), both of which have gone
through several editions. The Howard Taylors
also wrote HUDSON TAYLOR'S SPIRITUAL SECRET
(London: China Inland Mission, 1932). More
popular are Marshall Broomhall, HUDSON TAYLOR,
THE MAN WHO BELIEVED GOD(London: China In-
land Mission, 1929), and J. C. Pollock, HUDSON
TAYLOR AND MARIA: PIONEERS IN CHINA (London:
Hodder & Stoughton, 1962). Important is M.
Geraldine Guinness, (Mrs. F. H. Taylor) THE
STORY OF THE CHINA INLAND MISSION, 2 vols.
(London: Morgan & Scott, 1893-94).

From Taylor's own hand are A RETROSPECT (London: Morgan, 1894), and UNION AND COMMUNION:
OR THOUGHTS ON THE SONG OF SOLOMON (London:
Morgan & Scott, 1894), the latter first
printed in CHINA'S MILLIONS. The 1914 edition contains a foreword by J. Stuart Holden

C. G. Moore was with Taylor in China before
being forced to return to England by his
wife's illness. He then became the unidenti-
fied editor of LIFE OF FAITH and was thereby
responsible for the increased mission focus
of the periodical. Fred Mitchell, for some

time Home Director of The China Inland Mission, became chairperson of the Keswick Convention. Mitchell's biographer is Phyllis Thompson, CLIMBING ON TRACK: A BIOGRAPHY OF FRED MITCHELL (London: China Inland Mission, 1953).

Other accounts by men involved in the first beginnings of missionary awareness at Keswick were contributed to THE KESWICK CONVENTION, edited by Charles F. Harford (London: Marshall Bros., 1907). Eugene Stock contributed an essay entitled, "The Missionary Element," J. H. Battersby, "The Keswick Mission Council," and F. B. Meyer and Charles Inwood, "In Other Lands," the latter being a record of tours by Keswick speakers to lend spiritual and emotional support to missionaries on the field. Steven Barabas, SO GREAT SALVATION, is a significant source. See also John Pollock, THE KESWICK STORY (London: Hodder & Stoughton, 1964), for a popular account.

Additional material must be ferreted from biographies such as TEMPLE GAIRDNER OF CAIRO (London: S.P.C.K., 1930), by Constance Padwick; Archibald M. Hay, CHARLES INWOOD, HIS MINISTRY AND ITS SECRET (London: Marshall, 1929), and W. R. Wheeler, A MAN SENT FROM GOD: A BIOGRAPHY OF ROBERT E. SPEER[25] (Westwood, N.J.: Revell, 1956).

---

25.   Robert Elliott Speer, a member of the
        Student Volunteer movement (See Neill,
ed., CONCISE DICTIONARY OF THE CHRISTIAN
WORLD MISSION [Nashville: Abingdon, 1971],
pp. 571-572), and later senior secretary of
the Board of Foreign Missions of the Presbyterian Church in the U.S.A., was a popular
speaker at Keswick and at Moody's Northfield,
Winona Lake, Indiana, and other "Keswick"
conventions. A prolific author, he contributed to WINONA ECHOES, NORTHFIELD ECHOES and

The Missionary concerns are reflected today
by the many mission groups who recruit and
advertise at the Convention, by records of
missionary meetings published in the annual,
THE KESWICK WEEK, and by the multitude of
mission oriented articles appearing in the
weekly LIFE OF FAITH.

Conventions Abroad. LIFE OF FAITH continuously reports on "Keswick" conventions
throughout the world. John Pollock, THE KES-
WICK STORY (London: Hodder & Stoughton,
1964), p. 97, note 3, gives a list of several
"offshoots" with date of origin but is not
complete. SCOTLAND'S KESWICK: SKETCHES AND
REMINISCENCES (London: Marshall Bros., 1917),
by Norman C. Macfarlane chronicles the Convention there. THE MID-AMERICA KESWICK WEEK,
VITAL MESSAGES BY NINE CONTEMPORARY CHRISTIAN
LEADERS (Westwood, N.J.: Revell, 1960), is
the only published record of the meetings
held at Moody Memorial Church, Chicago since
1954. No registry of "Keswick" camps or conventions has been found.

THE FUNDAMENTALS (Vol. 3, 61-75; 12, 64-84).
His books focused on missions, ecclesiastical
unity and the internal life. See especially
the often reprinted, THE MARKS OF A MAN; OR,
THE ESSENTIALS OF CHRISTIAN CHARACTER (Cincinnati: Jennings & Graham, 1907); JESUS AND
OUR HUMAN PROBLEMS (N.Y.: Revell, 1946),
dealing with the relationship between Christ
and sin; THE MEANING OF CHRIST TO ME (N.Y.:
Revell, 1936), an exposition based on the
life of Christ; and THE FINALITY OF JESUS
CHRIST (N.Y.: Revell, 1933), given originally as the L.P. Stone Lectures at Princeton
Theological Seminary, 1932-1933 and The Gay
Lectures at the Southern Baptist Theological
Seminary, 1932-1933. See also K. S. Latourette, "Speer, Robert E." in Neill, CONCISE
DICTIONARY OF THE CHRISTIAN WORLD MISSION,
pp. 565-566.

The Keswick Movement began almost immediately
to influence the American religious scene.
Keswick had received its impetus from American revivalism via the Robert Pearsall Smiths,
W. E. Boardman, Asa Mahan, Amanda Smith and
A. T. Pierson. These men and women were of
the perfectionist persuasion and leaned more
toward Arminian than toward Calvinistic theological categories regarding Christian spirituality. They were oriented toward thinking
in "crisis" language. Literature and folk-
lore are the recorders of the excesses en-
gendered.

The British leaders, mainly Anglican, had a
moderating influence on religious crisis enthusiasm (see below, Theological Distinctives).
Moody,[26] who had been perceived as a co-

---

26. Dwight Lyman Moody was the subject of
     biographies by two of his sons. William
R. Moody, THE LIFE OF DWIGHT L. MOODY (N.Y.:
Revell, 1900), provided "The Official Authorized Version," complete with tributes by F. B.
Meyer and G. Campbell Morgan. Paul D. Moody,
MY FATHER; AN INTIMATE PORTRAIT OF DWIGHT
MOODY (Boston: Little, Brown, 1938), gives
a picture of Moody as the warm, lovable, vi-
tal human being, which balances the rather
stiff quaint man portrayed in his THE SHORTER
LIFE OF D. L. MOODY (Chicago: Bible Insti-
tute Colportage Association, 1900). Accounts
of Moody's work in Europe may be found in the
ponderous dusty chronicles of John Hall, THE
AMERICAN EVANGELISTS, D. L. MOODY AND IRA D.
SANKEY, IN GREAT BRITAIN AND IRELAND (N.Y.:
Dodd & Mead, 1875), as well as in Edgar Johnson Goodspeed, A FULL HISTORY OF THE WONDER-
FUL CAREER OF MOODY AND SANKEY, IN GREAT BRIT-
AIN AND AMERICA ...(N.Y.: Henry S. Goodspeed,
1876).

More recently, J. C. Pollock, MOODY: A BIO-
GRAPHICAL PORTRAIT OF THE PACESETTER IN MOD-

laborer in revival by Smith, was quick to
transport the restrained spiritual expression
of Keswick back to his famed Northfield Conferences and to what became Moody Bible
Institute in Chicago.[27] (Go to next page)

ERN MASS EVANGELISM (N.Y.: Macmillan, 1963),
the British edition entitled, MOODY WITHOUT
SANKEY; A NEW BIOGRAPHICAL PORTRAIT (London:
Hodder & Stoughton, 1963), has rewritten
the story of Moody's life, but the lack of
documentation makes it of little value for
research.

James F. Findlay's Ph.D. thesis at the University of Chicago, published as DWIGHT L. MOODY,
AMERICAN EVANGELIST, 1837-1899 (Chicago:
University of Chicago, 1969), is by far the
best work available on Moody. Also indispensable is Wilbur M. Smith, AN ANNOTATED BIBLI-
OGRAPHY OF D.L. MOODY (Chicago: Moody, 1948).
With the inevitable omissions that plague
such an effort, it is carefully done, including previously unpublished materials.

Of particular interest for the discussion of
Holiness Movement-Keswick relations is the
"sanctification" experience of D. L. Moody
alluded to in his own writings and discussed
by Sarah A. Cooke, a Free Methodist layperson,
in THE HANDMAIDEN OF THE LORD; OR, WAYSIDE
SKETCHES (Chicago: Arnold, 1896), revised
and enlarged as WAYSIDE SKETCHES; OR, THE
HANDMAIDEN OF THE LORD (Grand Rapids: Shaw,
n.d.). Moody's experience was also discussed
several times by Asa Mahan in DIVINE LIFF

27. Moody Bible Institute of Chicago, found-
     ed circa 1886, has been thoroughly stud-
ied by Gene A. Getz, MBI; THE STORY OF MOODY
BIBLE INSTITUTE (Chicago: Moody, 1969). A
careful effort is made to chronicle the out-
reach as well as the history of the institu-

R. A. Torrey,[28] Moody's choice for Director
of Chicago Bible Institute, spoke at Keswick;
Moody invited A.T. Pierson, H.W. Webb-Peploe,[29]

---

tion. The extensive bibliography, pp. 356-
369, must serve as a beginning for any additional research.

28. Reuben Archer Torrey had a varied career
      as evangelist, author, and Bible School
leader. Apparently no extensive critical bio-
graphical examination of Torrey's contribu-
tion has been made. John Kennedy Maclean pub-
lished three small volumes: TORREY AND ALEX-
ANDER, THE STORY OF THEIR LIVES (London:
Partridge, 1905), TRIUMPHANT EVANGELISM: THE
THREE YEARS' MISSIONS OF DR. TORREY AND MR.
ALEXANDER IN GREAT BRITAIN AND IRELAND (Lon-
don: Marshall Bros., 1905), and UNDER TWO
MASTERS: THE STORY OF JACOBY, DR. TORREY'S
ASSISTANT (London: Marshall Bros., 1905).
All are popular and devotional but not very
helpful for understanding the man himself.
Torrey was particularly influential in com-
bining the concern for personal holiness with
millenarian concerns. THE BAPTISM WITH THE
HOLY SPIRIT (N.Y.: Revell, 1895), and THE
FUNDAMENTAL DOCTRINES OF THE CHRISTIAN FAITH
(N.Y.: Doran, 1918), were his most important
books. An able tractarian, he focused more
and more on eschatology; e.g., THE RETURN OF
THE LORD JESUS; THE KEY TO THE SCRIPTURE, AND
THE SOLUTION OF ALL OUR POLITICAL AND SOCIAL
PROBLEMS; OR, THE GOLDEN AGE THAT IS SOON
COMING TO THE EARTH (Los Angeles: Bible In-
stitute of L.A., 1913). Several of Torrey's
sermons and the tract, "Why God Used D. L.
Moody," were often printed in holiness jour-
nals.

29. H. W. Webb-Peploe was a popular preacher
      at Keswick and Northfield. No major bi-
ography has been written. Barabas, SO GREAT

F. B. Meyer,[30] Andrew Murray,[31] and G. Camp-

SALVATION, pp. 165-169, is the most extensive
"vita." Most of his writings are from various convention addresses. Most influential
were his sermons, THE VICTORIOUS LIFE, and
THE LIFE OF PRIVILEGE: POSSESSION, PEACE,
AND POWER (London: Nisbet, 1896, 1897). For
additional bibliography see Jones, A GUIDE TO
THE STUDY OF THE HOLINESS MOVEMENT.

30. F. B. Meyer, "the best known Baptist
     clergyman of his day" (Barabas, SO GREAT
SALVATION, p. 182), was a vigorous proponent
of the Keswick message. Barabas (ibid., p.
186) observes, "It is doubtful whether any
other Keswick leader ever did more than Dr.
Meyer to make the distinctive Keswick message
known throughout the world." His life story
by W. Y. Fullerton, F. B. MEYER: A BIOGRAPHY
(London: Marshall, Morgan & Scott, 1929), is
a perceptive, highly readable account. M.
Jennie Street, F. B. MEYER: HIS LIFE AND
WORK (London: S. W. Partridge, 1902), is a
more popular account. See also Barabas, SO
GREAT SALVATION, pp. 182-186. The story of
his ministry at Leicester is found in F. B.
Meyer, THE BELLS OF IS; OR, VOICES OF HUMAN
NEED AND SORROW (London: Morgan & Scott,
1894). Here more than anywhere, the genius
of Meyer is revealed. An extensive listing
of his writings may be found in the advertise-
ments at the back of the book! A more traditional list, however, with incomplete bibliographic information and short title may be
found in chapter 24 of Fullerton

31. Andrew Murray, who spoke at "Keswick"
     meetings in America and England, spoke
most enduringly from his parish in South Africa through the pages of the SOUTH AFRICAN PI-
ONEER (see p. 82) and his often reprinted numerous books, pamphlets, and tracts. Of spe-

bell Morgan[32] to speak at Northfield. All
were prominent Keswick speakers. When in
1892 Moody was on an overseas crusade, A. J.
Gordon, Keswick speaker and Boston pastor,

---

cial significance are: THE SPIRIT OF CHRIST:
THOUGHTS ON THE INDWELLING OF THE HOLY SPIRIT
IN THE BELIEVER AND THE CHURCH (London: Nis-
bet, 1888; the American ed. of circa 1904 has
a biographical statement reprinted from the
SOUTH AFRICAN PIONEER); BACK TO PENTECOST:
THE FULFILLMENT OF "THE PROMISE OF THE FA-
THER" (ACTS 1:4) (London: Oliphants, 1918);
and HOLY IN CHRIST: THOUGHTS ON THE CALLING
OF GOD'S CHILDREN TO BE HOLY AS HE IS HOLY,
and THE TWO COVENANTS AND THE SECOND BLESSING
(London: Nisbet, 1888, 1889), in which are
set forth his concept of sanctification.
W. M. Douglas has summarized Murray's teaching in ANDREW MURRAY AND HIS MESSAGE: ONE OF
GOD'S CHOICE SAINTS (London: Oliphants,
1926); reprinted with some deletions, Fort
Washington, Pa.: Christian Literature Crusade, 1957. J. DuPlessis, THE LIFE OF ANDREW
MURRAY OF SOUTH AFRICA (London: Marshall
Bros., 1919), is a comparatively well written
biography. A valuable bibliography, unfortunately abbreviated, forms Appendix B, pp. 526
-535. The index is helpfully complete.

32. G. Campbell Morgan as a young man was
     rejected for ordination by the Wesleyan
Methodists. He became a popular and fre-
quent speaker both at Keswick and at Moody's
Northfield Conferences. John Harries,
G. CAMPBELL MORGAN, THE MAN AND HIS MINISTRY
(1930), is the best biography. Another, by
his daughter-in-law, Jill Morgan, is based on
his personal papers: A MAN OF THE WORD:
LIFE OF G. CAMPBELL MORGAN (1951). The
style, however, is awkward. THIS WAS HIS
FAITH: THE EXPOSITORY LETTERS OF G. CAMPBELL
MORGAN (1952), contains excerpts, topically

was left in charge of the meetings. Ernest
R. Sandeen,[33] THE ROOTS OF FUNDAMENTALISM:
BRITISH AND AMERICAN MILLENARIANISM, 1800-
1930 (Chicago: University of Chicago, 1970),
suggests that these meetings, and especially
F. B. Meyer, were influential in the adoption
of a Keswickian concern for a higher Christian life by the millenarians who were Calvinistic and conservative.

By 1913, an American Keswick Conference was
underway. Three volumes in particular are of
importance: VICTORY IN CHRIST: A REPORT OF
PRINCETON CONFERENCE 1916 (Philadelphia:
Board of Managers of Princeton Conf., 1916);
THE VICTORIOUS LIFE: MESSAGES FROM THE SUM-
MER CONFERENCES AT WHITTIER, CALIFORNIA, JUNE;
PRINCETON, NEW JERSEY, JULY; CEDAR LAKE, IN-
DIANA, AUGUST; INCLUDING ALSO SOME MESSAGES
FROM THE 1917 CONFERENCE AT PRINCETON AND
OTHER MATERIAL (Philadelphia: Board of Man-
agers of Victorious Life Conf., 1918), and THE
VICTORIOUS CHRIST: MESSAGES FROM CONFERENCES
HELD BY THE VICTORIOUS LIFE TESTIMONY IN 1922
(Philadelphia: Sunday School Times, 1923).
In the last volume is a brief historical

---

arranged. No data is included as to occa-
sion, recipient, etc. All the above were
published by Revell; each contains an incomplete list of his works. Harold Murray,
G. CAMPBELL MORGAN, BIBLE TEACHER: A SKETCH
OF THE GREAT EXPOSITOR AND EVANGELIST (London: Marshall, Morgan & Scott, 1938), is a
study on an important facet of Morgan's life.

33. Pp. 176-181, Sandeen, ROOTS OF FUNDAMEN-
TALISM is crucial for an understanding
of the deeper life movements within the U.S.
With careful precision he places the men and
issues in meaningful perspective. See especially Chapter 6, "The Prophecy and Bible
Conference Movement."

statement, "The Hour for America's Keswick" pps. 249-252, which ends in a plea for funds to support the new camp at Keswick, New Jersey.

The American Holiness Movement. While the Calvinistic branch of the deeper life movement was having considerable success in America, the Arminian branch was quickly losing its influence within Methodism and was being threatened by the successes of Pentecostalism, particularly in the South.[34] The sibling rivalry which developed has led to a hardening of both theological alternatives and to mutual caricature.

---

34. See C. E. Jones, PERFECTIONIST PERSUASION: THE HOLINESS MOVEMENT IN AMERICAN METHODISM 1867-1936, A.T.L.A. Monograph Series,5 (Metuchen, N.J.: Scarecrow, 1975). This superb book, based upon the heretofore mentioned, "Perfectionist Persuasion: A Social Profile of the National Holiness Movement Within American Methodism, 1867-1936" (Ph.D. dissertation, University of Wisconsin, 1968), is available from University Microfilms, Ann Arbor, Mich., number 68-0, 083). He discusses the origins of Nazarene, Free Methodist, Wesleyan, et al; churches. Vinson Synan, THE HOLINESS-PENTECOSTAL MOVEMENT IN THE UNITED STATES (Grand Rapids: Eerdmans, 1971), traces Pentecostal incursions in the American Holiness Movement. Additional bibliographic material necessary to understand this period may be found in the first two volumes of "Occasional Bibliographic Papers of the B. L. Fisher Library": Donald W. Dayton, THE AMERICAN HOLINESS MOVEMENT: A BIBLIOGRAPHIC INTRODUCTION, now undergoing substantial revision, and David W. Faupel, THE AMERICAN PENTECOSTAL MOVEMENT: A BIBLIOGRAPHIC ESSAY (Wilmore, Kentucky, Asbury Theological Seminary, 1971-1972).

The Holiness-Keswick debate focused on two
issues: original sin and the nature of sanctification. Holiness Movement clergy in the
Methodist-Wesleyan context emphasized the in-
stantaneous removal of original sin by an in-
stantaneous act of grace; viz, entire sanctification. Keswick maintained a Reformed view
of sin and a gradual process of sanctification. The categories became "eradicationist"
(Keswick term for the Holiness position) ver-
sus "suppressionist" (Holiness Movement term
for the Keswick position). Suppression described the Keswickian goal of "uniform sus-
tained victory over known sin." There was
agreement regarding the need for sanctification. The difference arose regarding its
meaning for the believer. It has been sug-
gested that Asa Mahan dropped out of the Keswick Convention after the first three; he re-
portedly observed at Brighton, "It doesn't
go deep enough."

W. B. Godbey,[35] radical Holiness Movement
preacher, teacher, and influential pamphlet-
eer, was one of the first to rise to the at-
tack. KESWICKISM (Louisville, Ky.: Pentecostal Publishing House, n.d.), discusses
the absoluteness of the destruction of sin,
then moves to an account of "My Keswickal Convention" in Madras, India. He comments on
the lack of spiritual power on the part of
those in attendance, observing:

        ...The truth of the matter is, their

---

35.   On William B. Godbey see his AUTOBIOGRA-
       PHY (Cincinnati: God's Revivalist Of-
fice, 1909), and his comments a year before
his death, HAPPY NONAGENARIAN (Zarephath, N.J.:
Pillar of Fire, 1919). For additional bibliography,though not complete, see Jones, A
GUIDE TO THE STUDY OF THE HOLINESS MOVEMENT.
A critical biography has not been published.

experience is simply a good case
of regeneration, as they only
claim to have sin suppressed and
kept down by grace in a subjugat-
ed state, so that it does not
break out and commit actual trans-
gression. (p. 48)...Keswickism is
a deficiency rather than a heresy
... (p. 59)...Keswickism as a nor-
mal consequence breaks down, because the Holy Ghost will not a-
bide, while old Adam remains in
the heart" (p. 61).

About 1910, A. M. Hills,[36] a Nazarene educa-
tor and writer, wrote SCRIPTURAL HOLINESS
AND KESWICK TEACHING COMPARED (Manchester:
Star Hall, n.d.), which for years has been
the standard Holiness Movement critique of
the Keswick Movement. Part I presents "Scriptural Holiness Teaching," arguing for a "second blessing" and "the eradication of car-
nality," and describing the reception and con-
tinuance in this "life of blessing" which is
"the longing of devout souls." Part II, "A
Review of Keswick Teaching," although undocu-
mented, features quotations from Keswick
speakers as reported in KESWICK WEEK. He com-
mends Keswick teachers for attempting to lift
the moral tone of the era, but notes that
"Keswick teachers are not consistent with
themselves, nor in agreement with each other,"
that their teaching is "painfully indistinct,"
that "much of what these preachers call holi-

---

36. Aaron Merritt Hills (1848-1935) supplied
     a short autobiographical statement to
PENTECOSTAL MESSENGERS (Cincinnati: M. W.
Knapp, 1898), and the FULL SALVATION QUARTERLY,
Vol. 5 (1899?). See also H. O. Wiley, "Dr.
A. M. Hills," HERALD OF HOLINESS, Vol. 40
(July 2, 1951), p. 388, and James McGraw,
"The Preaching of A. M. Hills," PREACHER'S
MAGAZINE, Vol. 33, No. 2 (1958), p.6-8.

ness is only regeneration," and that they
maintain an "unsound philosophy about self,
and the nature of flesh and depravity."
Hills' massive analysis lacks coherency, the
logic is often circular, and he clearly does
not understand the Keswick theological method and position. He furnishes a caricature
rather than an exposé of Keswickian teaching.

H. A. Baldwin,[37] a Free Methodist[38] pastor
and writer, published a curious little volume,
OBJECTIONS TO ENTIRE SANCTIFICATION CONSIDER-
ED (Pittsburgh: Published for the Author,
1911), containing short refutations to six-
teen "Objections." "Keswickism" is described
as "one of the most dangerous enemies of the
experience of holiness...for they give us to
understand that such a thing as the entire
eradication of the carnal nature from the
soul is an impossibility in this world" (p.
11). Quoting the famed Daniel Steele, Baldwin argues the Holiness Movement case on the
radical nature of New Testament language regarding sanctification and the eradication
of the carnal nature, but offers the amelio-
rating observation that only God knows the
heart of man!

The Keswickian perspective was asserted by

---

37. Harmon Allen Baldwin, OBJECTIONS TO
    ENTIRE-SANCTIFICATION CONSIDERED has re-
cently been reprinted by H. E. Schmul in HOL-
INESS CLASSICS, NO. I. (Titusville, Pa.:
The Allegheny Wesleyan Methodist Connection,
1973). Refer to C. E. Jones for biographical
and bibliographical data currently available.

38. For bibliographical direction on the
    Free Methodist Church, see Donald W. Day-
ton, THE AMERICAN HOLINESS MOVEMENT, A BIBLIO-
GRAPHIC INTRODUCTION and C. E. Jones, A GUIDE
TO THE STUDY OF THE HOLINESS MOVEMENT.

the indefatigable H. A. Ironside[39] in the often reprinted HOLINESS, THE FALSE AND THE
TRUE (New York: Loizeaux Brothers, 1912).
He chronicles, in fiercely polemical fashion,
his early frustrations as a member of the Salvation Army,[40] and attacks the level of spirituality within the Holiness Movement as a
unit. Moving from the autobiographical to
the doctrinal, Ironside argues for a progressive view of sanctification whereby the Christian comes to live victoriously over tempta-
tion and doubt: "All efforts to attain sinless perfection in this world can only end in
failure," (p. 132). "Only as one learns to
refuse everything that is of the flesh, and
finds everything in Christ, will...be enjoyed
a life lived in fellowship with God" (p. 133).

Henry E. Brockett, SCRIPTURAL FREEDOM FROM
SIN: A DEFENSE OF THE PRECIOUS TRUTH OF EN-
TIRE SANCTIFICATION BY FAITH AND AN EXAMINA-
TION OF THE DOCTRINE OF "THE TWO NATURES"
(Kansas City, Mo.: Nazarene, 1941), is pri-
marily a critique of Ironside's polemic. Re-
stating the classical American perfectionist
doctrine of entire sanctification, he relies
heavily upon A. M. Hills, SCRIPTURAL HOLI-
NESS AND KESWICK TEACHING COMPARED.

The controversy continued, often implicitly,
in the pulpits and periodicals of both per-

---

39. H. A. Ironside was a powerful American
     expositor and teacher. Closely identi-
fied with the American deeper life movement,
he was a frequent "Bible Camp" speaker and
for nineteen years, 1930-1948, was pastor of
Moody Memorial Church (THE MOODY CHURCH STORY,
n.d., n.p., 20 pps.), Chicago, the "campus"
church of Moody Bible Institute.

40. For bibliographical direction on The Sal-
     vation Army, see below under "Bibliogra-
phy." Dayton and Jones are particularly helpful.

spectives, although little of a scholarly nature was published until the 1960's, when the Holiness Movement began to wrestle with its identity, theologically and historically. Papers prepared originally for a National Holiness Association study group included George E. Failing, "Developments in Holiness Theology after Wesley" and Everett L. Cattell, "An Appraisal of the Keswick and Wesleyan Contemporary Positions," published as INSIGHTS INTO HOLINESS, compiled by Kenneth Geiger (Kansas City, Mo.: Beacon Hill, 1962). Both papers constitute cautious attempts to understand the relationship between Keswick and Holiness alternatives. Another of these papers was presented by W. Ralph Thompson to the Wesleyan Theological Society as "An Appraisal of the Keswick and Wesleyan Contemporary Positions," WESLEYAN THEOLOGICAL JOURNAL Vol. 1 (1966), p. 11-20. Thompson is more polemic but encourages the two sides to learn from each other:

> "Keswickism is weak in its scriptural foundation, but strong in its proclamation. Wesleyanism is doctrinally sound, but lacks in zeal and in positive presentation" (pp. 19-20).

More recently, Melvin E. Dieter, a Wesleyan,[41] has investigated the origins of the Keswick Movement, the early years of the subsequent revival and efforts at institutionalization within the various expressions of "Revivalism." Dieter presents by far the most balanced scholarly analysis from within the Holiness Movement.

The American Pentecostal Movement. Both W. B.

---

41.   For material relevant to The Wesleyan
      Church, see below: "Bibliography." Dayton and Dieter are especially helpful.

Godbey and A. M. Hills, who polemicized contra a Keswickian position, also lifted their
pens to refute Pentecostalism.[42]   David W.
Faupel, THE AMERICAN PENTECOSTAL MOVEMENT, A
BIBLIOGRAPHICAL ESSAY ("Occasional Bibliographic Papers of the B. L. Fisher Library," 2.
Wilmore, Ky.: Asbury Theological Seminary,
1972), originally published in the 1972 SUM-
MARY OF PROCEEDINGS: AMERICAN THEOLOGICAL
LIBRARY ASSOCIATION, lists fourteen Pentecostal denominations that do not subscribe to a
Wesleyan understanding of sanctification, but
adopt a Keswickian position. William Menzies
of Evangel College, Springfield, Missouri, in
1973 presented to the Society for Pentecostal
Studies, Cleveland, Tennessee, a paper entitled, "The Non-Wesleyan Origins of the Pentecostal Movement" (photocopy, 10 pps.). He
asserts that Alexander Dowie, A. B. Simpson,
founder of the Christian and Missionary Alliance and A. J. Gordon were influential in
the promotion of Keswick doctrines. He details (pages 5-9) the subsequent controversy
between Wesleyan and Keswickian types of holiness doctrine within Pentecostal groups.
Melvin Dieter read a paper before the Society
for Pentecostal Studies, Cleveland, Tennessee,
1973, "Wesleyan-Holiness Aspects of Pentecostal Origins: As Mediated through the Nineteenth Century Holiness Revivals" (30 pps.
photocopy), in which he traces the influence
of the Holiness Movement which, as noted a-
bove, also provided stimulus for the Keswick
Convention. Menzies' and Dieter's papers

---

42.   W. B. Godbey, SPIRITUAL GIFTS AND GRACES
      (Cincinnati: God's Revivalist Office,
1895), defines tongues as languages and encourages all to seek this "gift." Later, he
wrote the acidic TONGUE MOVEMENT, SATANIC
(Zarephath, N.J.: Pillar of Fire, 1918). A.
M. Hills wrote THE TONGUES MOVEMENT (Manchester,Eng.: Star Hall, 1910), to refute the
claims of the burgeoning Pentecostalism.

will soon be more readily available in a volume by Logos Press containing papers presented to the Society for Pentecostal Studies in
1972. The papers focus around the theme, "Aspects of Pentecostal Origins."

The Christian and Missionary Alliance. Note:
Publications mentioned in the following para-
graphs, except where otherwise indicated,
were published by the Christian Alliance, New
York, and currently by its successor, Christian Publications, Harrisburg, Pa. In 1974
the International Headquarters of the C. & M.
A. was moved from New York City to Upper Ny-
ack, New York. The Christian and Missionary
Alliance originated in the 1880's under the
direction of A. B. Simpson, pastor of 13th
Street Presbyterian Church in New York City.[43]
Frustrated in ministry and plagued by illness,
he was influenced by the faith healing and
millenarian hopes of A. J. Gordon,[44] THE MIN-

43. From 1887-1897 the Christian Alliance
     was Simpson's domestic association, and
The International Missionary Alliance was devoted to foreign missions. The "merger" produced the C. & M. A.

44. Adoniram Judson Gordon (1836-1895) was
     an influential Baptist in America and a
leader of the millenarian movement (Sandeen,
THE ROOTS OF FUNDAMENTALISM, passim). He ex-
ercised much influence in the early synthesis
of the C. & M. A., primarily through the book
mentioned above and through his often reprinted THE MINISTRY OF THE SPIRIT, with an introduction by F. B. Meyer (Philadelphia: American Baptist Pub. Soc., 1894). Also important
is THE TWOFOLD LIFE: OR, CHRIST'S WORK FOR US,
AND CHRIST'S WORK IN US (Boston: H. Gannett,
1883), a study in the attainment of "the abundant life." His autobiography is HOW CHIRST
CAME TO CHURCH; THE PASTOR'S DREAM: A SPIRIT-

ISTRY OF HEALING: OR, MIRACLES OF CURE IN ALL
AGES (Boston: H. Gannett, 1882), and W. E.
Boardman (see above, note 13). Concerned for
evangelism among the underprivileged both at
home and abroad, Simpson withdrew from the
Presbyterian Church, founding the new Alli-
ance around the fourfold doctrine of Christ
as Saviour, Sanctifier, Healer, and Coming
King. Simpson's writings emphasize these con-
cerns: THE FOUR-FOLD GOSPEL (1925), THE FUL-
NESS OF JESUS; OR CHRISTIAN LIFE IN THE NEW
TESTAMENT (1890), LIFE MORE ABUNDANTLY (1912),
WALKING IN THE SPIRIT (n.d.), WHOLLY SANCTI-
FIED (1925), THE GOSPEL OF HEALING (1915),
(all of the above are being made available in
paperback), THE LORD FOR THE BODY, WITH QUES-
TIONS AND ANSWERS ON DIVINE HEALING (1925),
an enlargement of the earlier THE DISCOVERY
OF DIVINE HEALING (1903), THE COMING ONE
(1912) and HEAVEN OPENED: OR, EXPOSITIONS OF
THE BOOK OF REVELATION (1899).

Simpson's life, chronicled by A. E. Thompson,
THE LIFE OF A. B. SIMPSON: WITH SPECIAL CHAP-
TERS BY PAUL RADER, JAMES M. GRAY, J. GREGORY
MANTLE, R. H. GLOVER, KENNETH MACKENZIE, F. H.
SENFT, AND W. M. TURNBULL (1920), was revised
as A. B. SIMPSON: HIS LIFE AND WORK (1939).
A. W. Tozer, WINGSPREAD: ALBERT B. SIMPSON,
A STUDY IN SPIRITUAL ALTITUDE (Centenary ed.,
1943), is an exposition of his life.

Studies of the historical development of the
Christian and Missionary Alliance are George
P. Pardington, TWENTY-FIVE WONDERFUL YEARS,
1889-1914: A POPULAR SKETCH OF THE CHRISTIAN

UAL AUTOBIOGRAPHY, BY A. J. GORDON...WITH THE
LIFE-STORY, AND THE DREAM AS INTERPRETING THE
MAN, BY A. T. PIERSON (Philadelphia: Amer.
Baptist Pub. Soc., 1895). His son,Ernest B.
Gordon, wrote ADONIRAM JUDSON GORDON, A BIOG-
RAPHY (New York: Revell, 1896).

AND MISSIONARY ALLIANCE (1914), and AFTER FIF-
TY YEARS: A RECORD OF GOD'S WORKING THROUGH
THE CHRISTIAN AND MISSIONARY ALLIANCE, by R.
B. Ekvall et al. (1939). Samuel J. Stoesz,
UNDERSTANDING MY CHURCH (1968), is intended
as a manual for church members and is a good
survey of history, doctrine and polity, unfor-
tunately without bibliography. J. H. Hunter's
75th anniversary volume was devoted to a
study of mission work, BESIDE ALL WATERS; THE
STORY OF SEVENTY-FIVE YEARS OF WORLD-WIDE MIN-
ISTRY: THE CHRISTIAN AND MISSIONARY ALLIANCE
(1964). Mission work is also chronicled in
MISSIONARY ATLAS: A MANUAL OF THE FOREIGN
WORK OF THE CHRISTIAN AND MISSIONARY ALLIANCE,
(4th ed., 1964; 1st ed. 1936).

The Christian and Missionary Alliance has produced significant missionary policy material;
for example, Louis L. King, "A Presentation
of the Indigenous Church Policy of the Christian and Missionary Alliance" (photocopy 17
pps., 1961?). They sponsored and published
the REPORT OF PROCEEDINGS of the Afro-Asia
Alliance Literature Conference, April, 1963
(1964),hoping to strengthen indigenous work.
A rich heritage of missionary biography includes Russell T. Hitt, CANNIBAL VALLEY (1962),
a story of Dutch New Guinea, and James C. Hefley, BY LIFE OR BY DEATH (Grand Rapids: Zondervan, 1969), about missionary efforts in
Indo-China.

The most influential theologian of the Christian and Missionary Alliance has been George
P. Pardington, THE CRISIS OF THE DEEPER LIFE[45]
(1906), who defined the Keswick orientation
toward sanctification to be adopted by the denomination. With his conciliatory language,

_____

45. Pardington, THE CRISIS OF THE DEEPER
      LIFE, along with several volumes by A. W.
Tozer have been reprinted in paperback by
Christian Pub., Harrisburg, Pa.

the Christian and Missionary Alliance has
been able to maintain close relationship with
the American Holiness Movement, although it
has remained outside the orb of the National
Holiness Association. It is particularly im-
pressive that the Christian and Missionary
Alliance did not develop a hostile polemic
contra Pentecostalism as did the Holiness
Movement, but maintains an attitude of "seek
not, forbid not" to this day. A. W. Tozer,
Oswald J. Smith, and of course, A. B. Simpson
have been the important Christian and Missionary Alliance expositors. For additional bibliography see C. E. Jones, A GUIDE TO THE
STUDY OF THE HOLINESS MOVEMENT, which contains the most complete bibliography to date
on the Christian and Missionary Alliance.

LITERATURE OF KESWICK

The literature produced under the impetus of
the Keswick Movement falls into three over-
lapping categories: theological, biblical,
and devotional studies. With regard to this
extensive corpus of literature, several problems arise. First, the Keswick Convention
in England has never defined a precise theological perspective. Rather, "Keswick theology" tends to revolve around a few "guiding
lights" who, in each generation, have managed
to keep on a track consistent with the heritage of the movement. Throughout, the concern has been for "practical holiness," for
the experience of the power of God within the
life of the believer. There is no creedal
statement, merely a rather remarkable consen-
sus of theological orientation. It is very
different in America. The American "Keswick"
people bought quickly and deeply into the Mil-
lenarian-Fundamentalist strictness of doctrine, while attempting to maintain the British experiential emphasis. R. A. Torrey, A.
T. Pierson, H. A. Ironside and F. B. Meyer
were involved in producing THE FUNDAMENTALS
(Chicago: Testimony Publishing House, 1910-

1915). R. A. Torrey together with A. C. Dixon and Louis Meyer edited this influential
series which continues to express the creed
of American fundamentalism. Thus, the rep-
resentatives of American "Keswick" tend to be
more concerned with correct (conservative)
thinking than with the experiential aspects
of the Christian life. Both American and British Keswickians endeavor to be "based on the
Bible."

The method of this portion of the essay is to
divide the literature according to its emphases. Theological Studies will present literature which addresses a concern of doctrine,
focusing on the issue. Devotional Studies
will be considered the work of authors who,
in summary or synthetic fashion, devote themselves to explicating Christian spirituality.
Biblical Studies involve major expositions,
commentaries and Bible study aids.

Bibliography

The Keswick Convention has not produced institutions which in turn would carefully define
what is to be considered "Keswick" or not
"Keswick." Keswick has remained a Convention,
that is, a loosely associated group concerned
with the deeper life, and has generally been
ignored by church historians. Thus the state
of bibliographic research is sadly lacking.
The Keswick Movement is not treated in the
various standard bibliographic tools;however,
THE BRITISH MUSEUM GENERAL CATALOGUE OF PRINT-
ED BOOKS is somewhat helpful in finding works
of a personage associated with the movement.
The bibliographic sources which are available
have been cited in the preceding section.

Theological Studies

Keswickian concern for "practical holiness"
began with a heavy emphasis on Christian experience, an inheritance left by the crusad-

ing American evangelists. W. E. Boardman
whose THE HIGHER CHRISTIAN LIFE, and IN THE
POWER OF THE SPIRIT were influential in Keswick origins, stressed a second crisis experience. Asa Mahan, THE BAPTISM OF THE HOLY
GHOST (New York: Palmer, 1870), and SCRIP-
TURE DOCTRINE OF CHRISTIAN PERFECTION (Boston:
D. S. King, 1839), later published as CHRIS-
TIAN PERFECTION (London: F. E. Longley,1875),
emphasized the possibility of immediate attainment of Christian perfection, as did
Robert Pearsall Smith, HOLINESS THROUGH FAITH,
LIGHT ON THE WAY OF HOLINESS. Although he
discounted sinless perfection, he retained
the experiential and crisis-oriented language.

The resulting excess of religious enthusiasm
was problematic for the early Keswick Convention as it sought acceptance for its participants and doctrines within the established
church. The American heritage was played
down and Keswickians began tracing their heritage to earlier authors(see above, note 4)
and especially to Walter Marshall, THE GOSPEL-
MYSTERY OF SANCTIFICATION, OPENED IN SUNDRY
PRACTICAL DIRECTIONS: SUITED ESPECIALLY TO
THE CASE OF THOSE WHO ARE UNDER THE GUILT AND
POWER OF INDWELLING SIN, TO WHICH IS ADDED A
SERMON ON JUSTIFICATION (Glasgow: Duncan and
Robertson, 1797), original London edition
1692, edited and reprinted by Andrew Murray
under the title, SANCTIFICATION, OR THE HIGH-
WAY OF HOLINESS (London: Nisbet, 1884). Marshall emphasized simplicity of faith and wait-
ing on Christ as requirements for sanctification, and the resultant joy and peace of
conscience. This book is devoid of the "religious enthusiasm" and "perfectionism" of the
later American writers, and draws heavily upon the Scriptures in explicating sanctification in a winsome nonpolemic manner.

Other competent Keswick leaders developed
and re-emphasized this approach to the issue.
H. C. G. Moule, THOUGHTS ON CHRISTIAN SANCTI-

TY (London: Seeley, 1885), (reprinted by Moody Press, Chicago, n.d.),consisting primarily of sermons delivered to the Cambridge University Church Society, presents a careful exposition of sanctification as self-surrender, and the personal power of "Jesus Christ who lives for me and in me" (p. 93). Moule,[46]

---

46. Handley Carr Glyn Moule, Principal of Ridley Hall, Cambridge and later successor of B. F. Westcott as Bishop of Durham had a much needed stabilizing effect on Keswick. His careful exegetical studies served to keep the Convention from excesses which might have destroyed its effectiveness. His biographers were Keswick men. John Harford Battersby and Frederick Charles Macdonald, HANDLEY CARR GLYN MOULE, BISHOP OF DURHAM, A BIOGRAPHY (London: Hodder & Stoughton, n.d. 1922?),is a rather traditional biography based on his letters and papers. John Baird, THE SPIRITUAL UNFOLDING OF BISHOP H. C. G. MOULE, D.D., AN EXPOSITION (London: Oliphants, n.d. 1926),is of little value, being primarily an apology for an evangelical perspective. See also the briefer notes in OXFORD DICTIONARY OF THE CHRISTIAN CHURCH, p. 930; DICTIONARY OF NATIONAL BIOGRAPHY 1912-1921, p. 390-391 and Barabas, SO GREAT SALVATION, 169-175. A complete list of his works can be found in Battersby and Macdonald. Of primary interest are JUSTIFYING RIGHTEOUSNESS (London: Seeley, 1885), OUTLINES OF CHRISTIAN DOCTRINE (London: Hodder & Stoughton, 1889), VENI CREATOR (London: Hodder & Stoughton, 1890), PHILIPPIAN STUDIES (London: Hodder & Stoughton, 1897), COLOSSIAN STUDIES (London: Hodder & Stoughton, 1898), EPHESIAN STUDIES (London: Hodder & Stoughton, 1900). NEED AND FULNESS (London: Marshall Bros., 1895),is a series of six addresses included in the KESWICK LIBRARY. PATIENCE AND COMFORT (1896) and CHRIST AND THE CHRISTIAN (1919) are addresses

through his books, as well as his frequent
appearances at the Keswick Convention, wielded a crucial, formative influence on the theological outlook of the Convention.

Alexander Smellie,[47] LIFT UP YOUR HEARTS:
FOUR ADDRESSES ON SANCTIFICATION (London: Andrew Melrose,1915), a volume dedicated to E-
van Hopkins, promotes the concept of achiev-
ing holiness through quiet surrender of self,
holiness which, "though it is perfect, it is
being perfected," (p. 65). However, Hopkins,
THE LAW OF LIBERTY IN THE SPIRITUAL LIFE
(1884), is the first orderly and extensive
analysis of the essentials of the Christian
life from a Keswickian perspective.

The Keswickian view of sin, first expounded
in print by Hopkins, has been given addition-
al exposition in H. C. G. Moule, NEED AND FUL-
NESS (London: Marshall Bros., 1894), and OUT-
LINES OF CHRISTIAN DOCTRINE (London: Hodder
& Stoughton, 1889), which, together with W. H.
Griffith Thomas,[48] THE PRINCIPLES OF THEOLO-

---

delivered at Keswick on the subject of the
Christian life and subsequently published by
Marshall Brothers.

47. Alexander Smellie, the biographer of Evan
     Henry Hopkins, was a prolific producer
of devotional material. GIVE ME THE MASTER
(London: Andrew Melrose, 1906), IN THE HOUR
OF SILENCE, A BOOK OF DAILY MEDITATIONS FOR
A YEAR (London: Andrew Melrose, 1899), LIFT
UP YOUR HEARTS, FOUR ADDRESSES ON SANCTIFICA-
TION (London: Andrew Melrose, 1915),and WAY-
FARERS' DAILY MESSAGE (London: Marshall, Mor-
gan & Scott, 1933-), are among his best pro-
ductions. See Pollock, THE KESWICK CONVEN-
TION, passim, for additional details.

48. William Henry Griffith Thomas has not
     yet been the subject of a biographer.

GY: AN INTRODUCTION TO THE THIRTY-NINE AR-
TICLES (London: Longmans, Green, 1930), and
R. W. Dale,[49] CHRISTIAN DOCTRINE (London:
Hodder & Stoughton, 1894), is about as close
to systematic theology as Keswickians have
attained. John Laidlaw, a professor of sys-
tematic theology at New College, Edinburgh,
worked with the problem of sin in THE BIBLE
DOCTRINE OF MAN: OR, THE ANTHROPOLOGY AND
PSYCHOLOGY OF SCRIPTURE (Edinburgh: Clark,
1879), and FOUNDATION TRUTHS OF SCRIPTURE AS
TO SIN AND SALVATION (Edinburgh: Clark,
1897). More popular in presentation are A.
T. Pierson, SHALL WE CONTINUE IN SIN? A VI-
TAL QUESTION FOR BELIEVERS ANSWERED IN THE
WORD OF GOD (London: Marshall Bros., 1897),
and Jessie Penn-Lewis, THE WARFARE WITH SATAN
AND THE WAY OF VICTORY (Leicester: "Over-
comer" Book Room, 1906), often reprinted.
Steven Barabas, SO GREAT SALVATION, and THE
KESWICK WEEK, unfortunately not indexed, con-
tain discussions of the nature of sin. Sev-
eral addresses from the latter were selected
and edited by Herbert F. Stevenson in KES-
WICK'S TRIUMPHANT VOICE: FORTY-EIGHT OUT-
STANDING ADDRESSES DELIVERED AT THE KESWICK
CONVENTION, 1882-1962 (London: Marshall, Mor-
gan & Scott, 1963), and KESWICK'S AUTHENTIC
VOICE: SIXTY-FIVE DYNAMIC ADDRESSES DELIVER-
ED AT THE KESWICK CONVENTION, 1875-1957 (Lon-
don: Marshall, Morgan & Scott, 1959). The
view of sin held unofficially by Keswick is
Reformed and Anglican, rather than the Wes-
leyan understanding of Mahan, Boardman, and
Arthur.

Some data is available in THE NEW INTERNATION-
AL DICTIONARY OF THE CHRISTIAN CHURCH, ed. J.
D. Douglas (Grand Rapids: Zondervan, 1974).
An ardent Anglican, he sought to serve his
church as a teacher and scholar.

49. A. W. W. Dale, THE LIFE OF R. W. DALE OF
    BIRMINGHAM (London: Hodder & Stoughton,

Quite understandably, the primary focus of
theological effort has been related to an understanding of the Holy Spirit and the Holy
Spirit's work in the believer's life; that
is, personal holiness. As mentioned above,
Moule, Smellie and Hopkins led the way in the
formulation of a Keswickian view of sanctification. Hopkins, THE LAW OF LIBERTY IN THE
SPIRITUAL LIFE views "Sanctification. ..as a
process; that is, as a work wrought in the
soul of the believer by the Holy Spirit, subsequently to regeneration." (p. 62) He quotes
"Owen on the Work of the Holy Spirit: 'It is
begun at once, and carried on gradually.'"
He sees sanctification as "a progressive and
gradual development of the new creation within the believer" (p. 63).

William MacDowall Aitken, THE HIGHWAY OF HOLI-
NESS: HELPS TO THE SPIRITUAL LIFE (London:
Shaw, 1883), picks up Hopkins' emphasis, warn-
ing against both spiritual dejection about
one's "state of grace" and antinomianism.
James Elder Cumming, "THROUGH THE ETERNAL
SPIRIT": A BIBLE STUDY ON THE HOLY GHOST
(Stirling: Drummond's Tract Depot, 1891),
is a lucid, more sophisticated treatment of
the nature and work of the Holy Spirit. H.
C. G. Moule contributed to the discussion,
VENI CREATOR: THOUGHTS ON THE PERSON AND
WORK OF THE HOLY SPIRIT OF PROMISE (London:
Hodder & Stoughton, 1890), an exposition on
personal holiness, and an anthology of ser-
mons, CHRIST IS ALL: SERMONS FROM NEW TESTA-
MENT TEXTS ON VARIOUS ASPECTS OF THE GLORY
AND WORK OF CHRIST (London: Sampson, Low,
1892), reprinted in the EXPOSITOR'S LIBRARY
(London: Hodder & Stoughton, 1912). Both

1898) is the biography by a son of this so-
cially concerned Congregationalist pastor-
theologian. See also OXFORD DICTIONARY OF
THE CHRISTIAN CHURCH, p. 369.

volumes represent a concern that the quest for Christian holiness occur within Christo-centric perceptions of the workings of God.

Written at the suggestion of, and dedicated to the memory of George H. C. MacGregor,[50] THE THINGS OF THE SPIRIT: TEACHING OF THE WORD OF GOD ABOUT THE SPIRIT OF GOD (London: Marshall Bros., 1898),is a Bible survey by G. Campbell Morgan. Morgan, THE SPIRIT OF GOD (New York: Revell, 1900), is an effort to re-interpret a Keswickian understanding of the Holy Spirit in light of the burgeoning dis-pensationalist model of the spiritual his-tory of the world. The latter work found pop-ularity primarily in America.

Andrew Murray, the prolific South African au-thor, who was introduced to the higher life by Bishop William Taylor of the Methodist Episcopal Church and a member of the National Holiness Association, has influenced greatly the development of spirituality within the deeper life movement of Europe and America by his often reprinted writings: ABSOLUTE SUR-RENDER AND OTHER ADDRESSES (New York: Revell, 1897); THE FULL BLESSING OF PENTECOST: THE ONE THING NEEDFUL (New York: Revell, 1908), a manual on being "filled with the Spirit of God"; THE SPIRIT OF CHRIST: THOUGHTS ON THE INDWELLING OF THE HOLY SPIRIT IN THE BELIEVER AND THE CHURCH (London: Nisbet, 1888); BE PERFECT! A MESSAGE FROM THE FATHER IN HEAVEN TO HIS CHILDREN ON EARTH (Chicago: Revell, 1894), in Revell's THE BLESSED LIFE SERIES featuring works of F. B. Meyer and Andrew Mur-ray; "LOVE MADE PERFECT" (London: Marshall Bros., 1894); and THE NEW LIFE (London: Nis-

---

50. The life-story is narrated by his son, Duncan Campbell MacGregor, GEORGE H. C. MACGREGOR, M. A., A BIOGRAPHY (London: Hod-der & Stoughton, 1900).

bet, 1891), revised and abridged by Bethany
Fellowship, Minneapolis, 1965, presenting
"the holy life of obedience and of fruitful-
ness in which the Holy Spirit teaches us to
walk" (p. 12).

F. B. Meyer, THE WAY INTO THE HOLIEST, EXPOSI-
TIONS OF THE EPISTLE TO THE HEBREWS (London:
Morgan & Scott, 1893), presents in sermons a
chronicle of the Christian progression toward holiness. THE CHRIST-LIFE FOR THE SELF-
LIFE, also published as A CASTAWAY (Chicago:
Bible Institute Colportage Association, 1897),
is a more conventional anthology on the holy
life.

During the somewhat troubled period following
the change of leadership from the "old-guard"
of Hopkins, Webb-Peploe and Moule to John
Harford,[51] son of John Harford Battersby, and
to J. Stuart Holden, literary production tap-
ered off as did the success of the Conventions in the tempestuous war era. From this
period of transition come J. Stuart Holden,
REDEEMING VISION, a study of the possibili-
ties of holy living, and THE PRICE OF POWER,
both published by Revell, 1908. W. H. Griffith Thomas, the remarkable scholar of the
holy life, contributed three important volumes. The most comprehensive, THE PRINCIPLES
OF THEOLOGY, AN INTRODUCTION TO THE THIRTY-
NINE ARTICLES (London: Longmans, Green, 1930),
published posthumously, presents a traditional Anglican-Keswickian conceptualization of
theology. Of excellent workmanship, it remains a valuable resource. THE HOLY SPIRIT
OF GOD (London: Longmans, 1913), is a thorough,

---

51.   Canon John Harford added Battersby to
      his Harford surname. Battersby was
dropped by most of his descendants. See C.
F. Harford, KESWICK CONVENTION (London: Marshall Bros., 1907), p. 51.

biblical, historical and systematic study of
the person and work of the Holy Spirit, originally given in 1913 as the L. P. Stone Lectures at Princeton Theological Seminary. Ap-
pended is a series of "Notes" on topics such
as tongues, laying on of hands, the baptism
of the Spirit, etc., and a bibliography, with
the overwhelming majority of titles referring
to Keswickian sources. Also see his THE ES-
SENTIALS OF LIFE (London: Pickering & Inglis,
1935), GRACE AND POWER: SOME ASPECTS OF THE
SPIRITUAL LIFE (New York: Revell, 1916), and
CHRISTIANITY IS CHRIST (London: Nisbet,
1909).

Of import far in excess of its modest size, W.
Graham Scroggie, THE FULNESS OF THE HOLY SPIR-
IT (Chicago: Bible Colportage Assn., 1925,
22 pps.),is an address given at the Moody Bi-
ble Institute of Chicago and published orig-
inally in the May 1925 issue of THE MOODY
MONTHLY. It is a concise summary of a Kes-
wickian understanding of sanctification.
Less concise, but of continuing influence in
Keswick circles is John Charles Ryle, HOLI-
NESS: ITS NATURE, HINDRANCES, DIFFICULTIES,
AND ROOTS (London: Hunt, 1879), reprinted
with an introduction by D. Martyn Lloyd-Jones
(London: Clarke, 1956).

Of momentous significance are three volumes
by J. Sidlow Baxter: A NEW CALL TO HOLINESS:
A RESTUDY AND RESTATEMENT OF NEW TESTAMENT
TEACHING CONCERNING CHRISTIAN SANCTIFICATION;
HIS DEEPER WORK IN US: A FURTHER INQUIRY IN-
TO NEW TESTAMENT TEACHING ON THE SUBJECT OF
CHRISTIAN HOLINESS; and OUR HIGH CALLING: A
SERIES OF DEVOTIONAL AND PRACTICAL STUDIES
IN THE NEW TESTAMENT DOCTRINE OF PERSONAL
SANCTIFICATION (London: Marshall, Morgan &
Scott, 1967). Summarizing and reformulating
in his lucid style, he observes, OUR HIGH
CALLING, p. 194, that sanctification, "is a
continuous inward renewing by the Divine Spir-
it, with a view to the transfiguration of

of character." All subsequent work will need to begin with Baxter.

There have been several works which have endeavored to express "the Keswick Position" on the issues of sin, consecration and sanctification. The earliest was THE KESWICK LIBRARY, including works by many prominent Keswick personalities. Published by Marshall Brothers, London, the LIBRARY consisted of: G. H. C. MacGregor, THE HOLY LIFE; F. S. Webster, THE SECRET OF HOLINESS; Evan H. Hopkins, HIDDEN, YET POSSESSED; F. B. Meyer, CALVARY TO PENTE-COST; Hubert Brooke, "THEY MIGHT BE." Jer. xiii.11; E. W. Moore, THE LIFE OF FELLOWSHIP; J. T. Wrenford, REALITY; Lucy Bennett, LIFTED LOADS; W. Houghton, THE SECRET OF POWER FOR DAILY LIVING; Sophia M. Nugent, "INSTEAD;" C. A. Fox,[52] VICTORY THROUGH THE NAME; C. G. Moore, "THINGS WHICH CANNOT BE SHAKEN." This LIBRARY, published 1894-1895, wielded considerable influence and individual volumes have been reprinted.

Charles Harford's anthology, THE KESWICK CONVENTION (London: Marshall Bros.), published in 1907, as the torch of leadership was being passed from the founding fathers to the second generation, contains a concise summary of the Keswick "message," written by H. C. G. Moule, Hubert Brooke, A. T. Pierson and J. B. Figgis. A. T. Pierson, FORWARD MOVEMENTS OF THE LAST HALF CENTURY (New York: Funk & Wagnalls, 1900), is also significant, chapter 3 being devoted to "Keswick Teaching," chapter 4 to "Keswick Method."

---

52. Fox, a prominent early Keswick leader, has been the subject of studies by Barabas, SO GREAT SALVATION and by Sophia M. Nugent, CHARLES ARMSTRONG FOX: MEMORIALS (London: Marshall Bros., 1901). For his role in Keswick, see also J. C. Pollock, THE KESWICK STORY.

Nothing, however, has had an impact comparable to Herbert F. Stevenson's four anthologies. The earliest, KESWICK'S AUTHENTIC VOICE (1959), and KESWICK'S TRIUMPHANT VOICE (1963), published by Zondervan, contain addresses delivered at the Keswick Convention from its earliest days. Both are organized around the foci: (1) Sin in the believer, (2) God's remedy for sin, (3) Consecration, and (4) The Spirit-filled life. Later collections, THE MINISTRY OF KESWICK: A SELECTION FROM THE BIBLE READINGS DELIVERED AT THE KESWICK CONVENTION, FIRST SERIES 1892-1919 (1963), and SECOND SERIES: 1921-1956 (1964), published by Zondervan, use similar categories for organization of material. These volumes provide significant information about Keswickian teaching.

Two additional aspects of Christian doctrine have been sporadically prominent, faith healing and eschatology, both having received more attention in American than in British circles. In America, A. J. Gordon, THE MINISTRY OF HEALING: OR,MIRACLES OF CURE IN ALL AGES (New York: Revell, 1882), reprinted in 1961 by Christian Publications, aroused widespread interest. Andrew Murray, DIVINE HEALING (New York: Christian Alliance, 1900), was reprinted in slightly altered form by Christian Literature Crusade in 1971. David Caradog Jones, SPIRITUAL HEALING: AN OBJECTIVE STUDY OF A PERENNIAL GRACE (London: Longmans, Green, 1955), is less than objective in its enthusiastic analysis. Jessie Penn-Lewis, of Welsh revival fame, contributed SOUL AND SPIRIT: A GLIMPSE INTO BIBLICAL PSYCHOLOGY (Bournemouth: Overcomer Book Room, n.d.). S. D. Gordon, QUIET TALKS ABOUT THE HEALING CHRIST (New York: Revell, 1924), is a study of "some principles of healing as taught in God's Word, directly and indirectly" (p. 5). Admiral E. Gardiner Fishbourne, WHOLENESS: OR, HOLINESS AND HEALTH THROUGH FAITH IN THE LORD JESUS CHRIST (London:

Stock, 1882), is prefaced by an essay "Faith Healing No New Doctrine" by Asa Mahan who argues that healing has long been a reputable practice within the church.

Efforts in analysis of the eschaton among early Keswick leaders consisted primarily of sermons, such as, H. W. Webb-Peploe, HE COMETH! (London: Marshall Bros., 1905), J. Stuart Holden, "BEHOLD, HE COMETH!" ADDRESSES ON THE SECOND COMING OF OUR LORD (London: Morgan & Scott, 1918), and H. C. G. Moule, CHRIST'S WITNESS TO THE LIFE TO COME AND OTHER SERMONS (London: Seeley, 1908). These, as the more sophisticated study of R. W. Dale, CHRIST AND THE FUTURE LIFE (4th ed. London: Hodder & Stoughton, 1902), are in continuity with the traditional understanding of the Christian church. More heavily influenced by the burgeoning enthusiasm for dispensationalism[53] were G. Campbell Morgan, GOD'S METHODS WITH MAN IN TIME: PAST, PRESENT, AND FUTURE (New York: Revell, 1898), complete with folded colored chart!; SUNRISE. "BEHOLD, HE COMETH!" AN INTRODUCTION TO A STUDY OF THE SECOND ADVENT (New York: Revell, 1912), originally preached as sermons; and William Graham Scroggie, RULING LINES OF PROGRESSIVE REVELATION (London: Marshall Bros., 1918). Also of interest is Herbert Stewart, THE STRONGHOLD OF PROPHECY: IRREFUTABLE EVIDENCE FROM FULFILLED PROPHECY THAT THE SCRIPTURES

---

53. Essential for understanding the complex matrix of millenarian dispensationalism of the early twentieth century is Ernest Sandeen, THE ROOTS OF FUNDAMENTALISM: BRITISH AND AMERICAN MILLENARIANISM, 1800-1930 (Chicago: Univ. of Chicago, 1969). Also helpful, primarily for bibliographies and for summaries of positions is Arnold D. Ehlert, A BIBLIOGRAPHIC HISTORY OF DISPENSATIONALISM (Grand Rapids: Baker, 1965).

ARE THE INFALLIBLE WORD OF GOD (London: Marshall, Morgan & Scott, 1935), endorsed by R.
H. Stephens Richardson, Chairman of the North
Ireland (Keswick) Convention, which begins
with a lengthy quotation from C. I. Scofield.

Moody's heirs, perhaps more than Moody himself, have influenced every aspect of American religious life and thought. The higher
life movement of which he was the most spec-
tacular example has to a great extent defined what are the accepted patterns of
thought and behavior for the typical conservative American Christian. This phenomenon
can be considered here only as it revolves
around The Moody Bible Institute. There are,
however, a myriad of Bible schools, insti-
tutes, Bible training centers, denominations,
colleges and associations which espouse the
Moody model. Although perhaps not its most
enthusiastic participant, MBI has provided a
seed-bed for the "Evangelical Awakening" of
the second half of the twentieth century.

Moody himself wrote two volumes which present
a Keswickian understanding of sanctification,
both published in Chicago by Revell: SECRET
POWER: OR, THE SECRET OF SUCCESS IN CHRIS-
TIAN LIFE AND CHRISTIAN WORK (1881), often
reprinted and, THE WAY TO GOD AND HOW TO FIND
IT (1884). R. A. Torrey,recipient of Moody's
"mantle," wrote extensively on the Spirit-
directed life. THE BAPTISM WITH THE HOLY
SPIRIT (New York: Revell, 1895), is thoroughly Keswickian rather than Wesleyan, progressive rather than crisis-oriented in emphasis.
HOW TO OBTAIN FULNESS OF POWER IN CHRISTIAN
LIFE AND SERVICE (London: Nisbet, 1897), is
a study designed for laymen, while the fol-
lowing are more technical in expression: THE
HOLY SPIRIT, WHO HE IS AND WHAT HE DOES AND
HOW TO KNOW HIM IN ALL THE FULNESS OF HIS GRA-
CIOUS AND GLORIOUS MINISTRY (New York: Re-
vell, 1927), and THE PERSON AND WORK OF THE
HOLY SPIRIT AS REVEALED IN THE SCRIPTURES AND

IN PERSONAL EXPERIENCE (New York: Revell,
1910), reprinted by Zondervan.

Ironside's anti-Wesleyan-Holiness polemic,
HOLINESS, THE FALSE AND THE TRUE has been mentioned.   More positive is THE MISSION OF THE
HOLY SPIRIT; AND, PRAYING IN THE HOLY SPIRIT
(combined ed.:   New York: Loizeaux Bros.,
1950).   Although not directly associated
with Moody Church or Moody Bible Institute,
James H. McConkey, THE THREE-FOLD SECRET OF
THE HOLY SPIRIT (Pittsburgh, Pa.:   Silver,
1897), reprinted by Moody, was well received
and translated into at least twenty languages.
McConkey was an able tractarian.   His best
are THE ABUNDANT LIFE, GUIDANCE, and LAW AND
GRACE, still available from "Back to the Bible," Lincoln, Nebraska.   A close friend of
McConkey, Robert C. McQuilkin, published
"What is Pentecost's Message Today?" in THE
SUNDAY SCHOOL TIMES and later reprinted it as
THE BAPTISM OF THE SPIRIT: SHALL WE SEEK IT?
(Columbia, S. C.: Columbia Bible College,
1935), which attacks both Pentecostalism and
"dead orthodoxy."   William Culbertson, pres-
ident of Moody Bible Institute and speaker at
both American and British Keswick conventions,
has contributed GOD'S PROVISION FOR HOLY LIV-
ING (Chicago: Moody, 1957), and THE FAITH
ONCE DELIVERED (Chicago: Moody, 1972).

An intense concern of the American higher
life movement, however, was eschatology and
prophecy.   Sandeen, ROOTS OF FUNDAMENTALISM,
chronicles the development of millenarianism
and the role of Keswickians, Moody and Scofield within that movement.   C. I. Scofield,
founder of Dallas Theological Seminary, was
the synthesizer of this material in the SCO-
FIELD BIBLE.   See also his ADDRESSES ON PRO-
PHECY (New York: Gaebelein, 1910).

H. A. Ironside, THE LAMP OF PROPHECY, OR
SIGNS OF THE TIMES (Grand Rapids: Zondervan,
1940), followed Scofield's outline while en-

deavoring to avoid extreme positions. Also
dispensational in nature was Donald Grey Barnhouse, TEACHING THE WORD OF TRUTH (Philadelphia: Revelation Book Service, 1940). More
recently, Wilbur M. Smith, YOU CAN KNOW THE
FUTURE (Glendale, Calif.: Regal Books, 1971),
and J. Dwight Pentecost, WILL MAN SURVIVE?
and PROPHECY FOR TODAY, along with the European scholar René Pache, THE FUTURE LIFE,
translated by Helen I. Needham (Chicago:
Moody, 1962),have been influential in this
area.

A. B. Simpson, THE FOUR-FOLD GOSPEL (New York:
Christian Alliance, 1890), reprinted with introduction by F. H. Senft in 1925, placed in
perspective the four-fold theological emphases of the Christian and Missionary Alliance:
the proclamation of Christ as Saviour, Sanctifier, Healer and Coming King.

Regarding Christ as Saviour, see A. B. Simp-
son, THE NAMES OF JESUS (New York: Christian
Alliance, 1892), and THE FULNESS OF JESUS; OR,
CHRISTIAN LIFE IN THE NEW TESTAMENT (New York:
Christian Alliance, 1890). The Keswickian al-
ternative of sanctification[54] was predominant
in the writings of A. B. Simpson, G. P.
Pardington, A. W. Tozer and Oswald J. Smith.
Simpson accomplished a major study, THE HOLY
SPIRIT: OR, POWER FROM ON HIGH, AN UNFOLDING
OF THE DOCTRINE OF THE HOLY SPIRIT IN THE OLD
AND NEW TESTAMENTS (2 vols.; New York: The
Christian Alliance, 1896). WHOLLY SANCTIFIED
and A LARGER CHRISTIAN LIFE are more system-
atic presentations of his views which were
reformulated by George P. Pardington, THE
CRISIS OF THE DEEPER LIFE.

---

54. The Wesleyan understanding of entire
     sanctification still has support in the
C. & M. A., probably because of its continuing contacts with the HOLINESS MOVEMENT and

Aiden Wilson Tozer, Simpson's successor, has
published several items about the holy life
(published by Christian Publications, Harris-
burg, except where otherwise noted): KEYS TO
THE DEEPER LIFE from the series in CHRISTIAN
LIFE (Grand Rapids: Zondervan, 1957); OF GOD
AND MEN (1960), in non-technical format; HOW
TO BE FILLED WITH THE HOLY SPIRIT, a series
of sermons; and THE KNOWLEDGE OF THE HOLY;
THE ATTRIBUTES OF GOD: THEIR MEANING IN
CHRISTIAN LIFE (New York: Harper, 1961), his
most famous work. Also sermonic is THE ROOT
OF THE RIGHTEOUS (1955).

Oswald J. Smith, founder and longtime pastor
of the famed Peoples Church of Toronto, Canada, is a prolific writer. His best materials focusing upon the issue of sanctification
are THE ENDUEMENT OF POWER (1933), revised in
1962, THE SPIRIT AT WORK (1939) and THE LORD
IS CALLING (1937), all published by Marshall,
Morgan & Scott, London.

Christ, the Healer, was the focus of A. J.
Gordon, MINISTRY OF HEALING which led Simpson
to an experience of healing and the writing
of THE DISCOVERY OF HEALING,THE GOSPEL OF
HEALING and LORD FOR THE BODY. Oswald J.
Smith, THE GREAT PHYSICIAN (New York: Chris-
tian Alliance, 1927), and Thomas J. McCrossan,
BODILY HEALING AND THE ATONEMENT (Seattle:
McCrossan, 1930), also reflect the concern
for healing.

A. B. Simpson, THE GOSPEL OF THE KINGDOM (2nd
ed.; 1890) is a vaguely premillennialist anal-
ysis based on a series of sermons, as is HEAV-
EN OPENED: EXPOSITIONS OF THE BOOK OF REVELA-
TION, in the CHRIST IN THE BIBLE series, Vol.
XXIV (1899). EPISTLES OF THE ADVENT; OR, THE

---

the number of clergy who have attended Asbury
College and Asbury Theological Seminary.

BLESSED HOPE IN THESSALONIANS (n.d.) and THE
COMING ONE (1912) are biblical-theological
studies, while more allegorical is BACK TO
PATMOS; OR, PROPHETIC OUTLOOK ON PRESENT CON-
DITIONS (1914). All these were published by
the Christian Alliance, now Christian Publications, Harrisburg, Pennsylvania.

George Palmer Pardington, the best theologian
of the Christian & Missionary Alliance em-
phasized a pre-millennial dispensationalist ap-
proach in OUTLINE STUDIES IN CHRISTIAN DOC-
TRINE (New York: Christian Alliance, 1916).
Oswald J. Smith, with more enthusiasm than
discretion published IS THE ANTICHRIST AT
HAND? (3rd ed., Toronto: Tabernacle Publish-
ers, 1926), an analysis of Mussolini; and
WHEN THE KING COMES BACK (London: Marshall,
Morgan & Scott, 1957), with an introduction
by Wilbur M. Smith, who himself wrote, WORLD
CRISES AND THE PROPHETIC SCRIPTURES (Chicago:
Moody, 1950), all now hopelessly out of date!
Oswald J. Smith, THE CLOUDS ARE LIFTING,
(n.d.), studies in prophecy and the visions
of Daniel, and PROPHECY - WHAT LIES AHEAD?
(1943, 1945, 1947, 1952), both published by
Marshall, Morgan & Scott, are more cautious
in prognostication and analogy.

For bibliographical hints concerning the theological perspective of the Pentecostals and
the Holiness Movement see Faupel, THE AMERI-
CAN PENTECOSTAL MOVEMENT and Dayton, THE AMER-
ICAN HOLINESS MOVEMENT. Within Methodism the
trend of the twentieth century was away from
a Wesleyan perfectionist understanding and toward a Keswickian perception of sanctification. Exemplary of this move is James Mudge,[55]

---

55. Mudge's own "testimony" appears in FORTY
     WITNESSES, COVERING THE WHOLE RANGE OF
CHRISTIAN EXPERIENCE, edited by S. Olin Garrison (New York: Hunt & Eaton, 1888). More

GROWTH IN HOLINESS TOWARD PERFECTION: OR,
PROGRESSIVE SANCTIFICATION (1895), which was
viciously attacked by the perfectionist stal-
wart, Daniel Steele, A DEFENSE OF CHRISTIAN
PERFECTION: OR, A CRITICISM OF DR. JAMES
MUDGE'S "GROWTH IN HOLINESS TOWARD PERFECTION"
(1896), and by Lewis Romaine Dunn, A MANUAL
OF HOLINESS AND REVIEW OF DR. JAMES B. MUDGE
(1895). Mudge replied by, THE PERFECT LIFE
IN EXPERIENCE AND DOCTRINE: A RESTATEMENT,
WITH INTRODUCTION BY REV. WILLIAM F. WARREN
(1911). All these titles were published in
New York by Hunt & Eaton or Eaton & Mains,
and in Cincinnati by Cranston & Curts, et al.

Alexander Alonzo Phelps, PURITY AND POWER: OR,
THE TWELVE P'S, A RADICAL AND SCRIPTURAL
TREATMENT OF THE DOCTRINE, EXPERIENCE AND
PRACTICE OF CHRISTIAN PERFECTION (Boston: Ad-
vent Christian, 1905), is a work by a Metho-
dist Episcopal writer who draws upon and rec-
ommends both the perfectionist holiness and
Keswickian writings of Daniel Steele and F.
B. Meyer.

Biblical Studies

Participants at the Keswick Convention have
been predominantly pastors, evangelists, missionaries, and Bible school faculty, rather
than academicians. This fact is reflected in
the biblical studies of Keswick men. These
works were seldom seminal, but served to en-
courage a greater degree of personal Bible
study or to indicate support for their theological perspective--at a lay level. The effectiveness of this approach may be seen by
the wide distribution the literature has received, and by the extensive support their
critical-theological positions have received

---

technical biographical data may be traced
through Jones, A GUIDE TO THE STUDY OF THE
HOLINESS MOVEMENT, p. 707.

from laity and clergy of all denominations in England and America.

The philosophical concepts controlling their exposition can be found in W. Graham Scroggie, IS THE BIBLE THE WORD OF GOD? (Philadelphia: Sunday School Times, 1922), answered affirmatively in the outline: "It seems to be; It claims to be; It proves to be." Scroggie delivered Bible readings at the Keswick Convention twelve times. Hubert Brooke, "Is the Bible Inspired?" in CAN WE TRUST THE BIBLE? CHAPTERS ON BIBLICAL CRITICISM (London: The Religious Tract Society, 1908), pps. 1-35, defended his thesis by analysis of prophecy and personal experience. A. T. Pierson, THE BIBLE AND SPIRITUAL CRITICISM (New York: Baker & Taylor, 1905), delivered first as the Exeter Hall Lectures on the Bible, is a defense of what would become the Fundamentalist approach to scripture. W. H. Griffith Thomas, "Old Testament Criticism and New Testament Christianity," in BACK TO THE BIBLE: THE TRIUMPHS OF TRUTH, by A. C. Dixon, et al. (London: Partridge, 1912), pp. 77-102, maintains that "the old is better" in response to the newly-arrived-in-America higher criticism.

No one was a more severe critic of higher criticism than R. A. Torrey, who for that reason was chosen by Moody to preside over the Chicago (later, Moody) Bible Institute. DIFFICULTIES AND ALLEGED ERRORS AND CONTRADICTIONS IN THE BIBLE (New York: Revell, 1907), TEN REASONS WHY I BELIEVE THE BIBLE IS THE WORD OF GOD (Chicago: Bible Inst. Colportage Assn., 1898), and especially THE HIGHER CRITICISM AND THE NEW THEOLOGY: UNSCIENTIFIC, UNSCRIPTURAL, AND UNWHOLESOME (Montrose, Pa.: Montrose Christian Literature Soc., 1911), defined the American Keswickian approach to scripture. As is obvious from the authors cited, the nature of scripture was a far greater issue in America than in Britain, and continues to be so. Rene Pache, THE INSPIRA-

TION AND AUTHORITY OF SCRIPTURE, translated by
Helen I. Needham (Chicago: Moody, 1969), continues in the same tradition.

A. T. Pierson, THE BIBLE AND SPIRITUAL LIFE
(London: Nisbet, 1908), is an effort to show
the practical nature of the scripture and the
virtue of personal Bible study. The emphasis
of Keswick on both sides of the Atlantic has
been to study the text as it stands rather
than to engage in higher criticism. This has
led to "How to" manuals exemplified by R. A.
Torrey, HOW TO STUDY THE BIBLE FOR GREATEST
PROFIT (London: Nisbet, 1896); THE IMPOR-
TANCE AND VALUE OF PROPER BIBLE STUDY (Chica-
go: Moody, 1921); THE NEW TOPICAL TEXT BOOK;
A SCRIPTURE TEXT BOOK FOR THE USE OF MINIS-
TERS, TEACHERS, AND ALL CHRISTIAN WORKERS.
WITH AN INTRODUCTION ON METHODS OF BIBLE STU-
DY BY REV.R. A. TORREY (New York: Revell,
1897); and introductions to the Bible such as
W. Graham Scroggie, [56] KNOW YOUR BIBLE, A
BRIEF INTRODUCTION TO THE SCRIPTURES, 2 vols.
(London: Pickering & Inglis, 1940; revised
1953; often reprinted), Scroggie, THE UNFOLD-
ING DRAMA OF REDEMPTION; THE BIBLE AS A WHOLE,
3 vols. (London: Pickering & Inglis, 1953-
1970), is a "synthetic" approach, interpret-
ing the Bible as one integral unit.

The commentator par excellence was William
Henry Griffith Thomas, whose work greatly influenced evangelical Anglicanism as well as
the Keswick Convention. On a methodological

---

56. W. G. Scroggie still holds the record
for Bible readings at the Keswick Convention: twelve between 1914 and 1954. THE
STORY OF A LIFE IN THE LOVE OF GOD, incidents
collected from the diaries of Mrs. James J.
(Jane) Scroggie and edited by her son, Dr. W.
Graham Scroggie (London: Pickering & Inglis,
1939) provides insights to Scroggie himself.

level are HOW WE GOT OUR BIBLE AND WHY WE BE-
LIEVE IT IS GOD'S WORD (Chicago: Moody,
1926), METHODS OF BIBLE STUDY (Chicago: Bible Inst. Colportage Assn., 1924), and HOW TO
STUDY THE FOUR GOSPELS (Philadelphia: Sunday
School Times, 1924). Thomas contributed the
following to A DEVOTIONAL COMMENTARY SERIES,
edited by A. R. Buckland and published by the
Religious Tract Society, London: GENESIS, 3
vols., reprinted as one volume (Grand Rapids:
Eerdmans, 1946), ROMANS, 3 vols. (reprinted
as one volume by Eerdmans, 1946), dedicated
to H. C. G. Moule, who contributed the volume, II TIMOTHY to the same series. Much of
the material of Thomas, THE ACTS OF THE APOS-
TLES: OUTLINE STUDIES IN PRIMITIVE CHRIS-
TIANITY (Chicago: Moody, 1939), was incorporated in OUTLINE STUDIES IN THE ACTS OF THE
APOSTLES (Eerdmans, 1956), edited by his
daughter who also edited his OUTLINE STUDIES
IN THE GOSPEL OF LUKE (Eerdmans, 1950), and
THROUGH THE PENTATEUCH CHAPTER BY CHAPTER
(Eerdmans, 1957).

Influential since the early era of the Conven-
tion has been H. C. G. Moule, THE EPISTLE OF
ST. PAUL TO THE ROMANS, EXPOSITOR'S BIBLE
SERIES (London: Hodder & Stoughton, 1894),
often reprinted, and the more scholarly vol-
ume in "The Cambridge Bible for Schools and
Colleges," THE EPISTLE OF PAUL THE APOSTLE TO
THE ROMANS (Cambridge: Univ. Press, 1899).

W. G. Scroggie commented on THE PSALMS, 4
vols. (London: Pickering & Inglis, 1948).
On the Acts of Apostles, commentaries were of-
fered by A. T. Pierson, THE ACTS OF THE HOLY
SPIRIT, dedicated to A. J. Gordon (London:
Marshall, Morgan & Scott, 1913), G. Campbell
Morgan, THE ACTS OF THE APOSTLES (New York:
Revell, 1924), and A. Q. Morton and G. H. C.
MacGregor, THE STRUCTURE OF LUKE AND ACTS
(New York: Harper & Row, 1964). On Romans,
in addition to those mentioned above, there
are commentaries by A. B. Simpson, THE EPIS-

TLE TO THE ROMANS (Harrisburg, Pa.: Christian Publications, n.d.), and Robert C. McQuilkin, THE MESSAGE OF ROMANS: AN EXPOSITION (Grand Rapids: Zondervan, 1947).

The Keswickians have been prolific and good Bible expositors. H. A. Ironside has published, through Loizeaux Brothers, notes on Proverbs, Ezra, Nehemiah, Esther, Jeremiah and Lamentations, the Minor Prophets, Daniel, the Revelation and Philippians, all of which have gone through several printings. F. B. Meyer published expositions on most books of the Bible. There is not space to list all of them. The best is THE EPISTLE TO THE PHILIPPIANS: A DEVOTIONAL COMMENTARY (London: Religious Tract Society, 1906). More recent are the works of John R. W. Stott, THE EPISTLES OF JOHN, TYNDALE NEW TESTAMENT COMMENTARIES, Vol. 19 (Grand Rapids: Eerdmans, 1964), THE MESSAGE OF GALATIANS (London: Inter-Varsity , 1968), GUARD THE GOSPEL: THE MESSAGE OF II TIMOTHY (Downers Grove, Ill.: Inter-Varsity, 1973), and Herbert F. Stevenson, THREE PROPHETIC VOICES: STUDIES IN JOEL, AMOS, AND HOSEA (1971), and JAMES SPEAKS FOR TODAY (1966),both by Marshall, Morgan & Scott.

Still less technical are numerous Bible addresses. Sir Stevenson Arthur Blackwood,[57] HEAVENLY PLACES. ADDRESSES ON THE BOOK OF JOSHUA (London: Nisbet, 1872), and THINGS WHICH GOD HATH JOINED TOGETHER: ADDRESSES ON ISAIAH XLV. 21-25 (London: Nisbet, 1878); Charles A. Fox, THE SPIRITUAL GRASP OF THE EPISTLES; OR, AN EPISTLE A-SUNDAY (London: Partridge, 1894); George Goodman, THE EPISTLE OF ETERNAL LIFE: AN EXPOSITION OF THE FIRST EPISTLE OF JOHN (London: Pickering & Inglis, 1936); A. T. Pierson, HIS FULNESS: FOUR BI-

---

57. Blackwood was one of Robert Pearsall
    Smith's supporters who became a leading
Keswick Convention personality. See Lady

BLE READINGS GIVEN AT KESWICK IN 1904 ON I
CORINTHIANS I.30 (London: Marshall Bros.,
1904); and W. H. Griffith Thomas, "LET US GO
ON:" THE SECRET OF CHRISTIAN PROGRESS IN THE
EPISTLE TO THE HEBREWS (London: Morgan &
Scott, 1923). The best of the Bible readings
at the Keswick Convention have been edited by
H. F. Stevenson in THE MINISTRY OF KESWICK.

Sermonic and Devotional Studies

The greatest contribution of the Keswick Convention and the higher life movement has been
the literature explicating Christian spirituality or devotional literature. Almost every
Keswick speaker of note has published a volume of sermons, the largest collection being
that of G. Campbell Morgan, THE WESTMINSTER
PULPIT, 10 vols. (New York: Revell, 1954-
1955), with a topical-textual index published
separately in 1954. THE TOZER PULPIT, 5 vols.
to date, edited and compiled by Gerald B.
Smith (Harrisburg, Pa.: Christian Publications, 1968-), is a major effort to preserve
the sermons of the great Christian and Missionary Alliance preacher. THE KESWICK WEEK
prints annually the sermons, Bible readings
and homilies delivered at the Keswick Convention.

According to some canons of evaluation, all
of the literature discussed above might be
considered "devotional." In a sense that is
true for the goal of Keswick, "the promotion
of practical holiness"--always somewhat intro-
spective--has resulted in a richness of spiritual roadmaps for progress in Christian ma-
turity. To list all literature would be far
beyond the scope of this essay, and to assert
that those mentioned below are the best would

Stevenson Arthur Blackwood, SOME RECORDS OF
THE LIFE OF STEVENSON ARTHUR BLACKWOOD, K. C.
B. (London: Hodder & Stoughton, 1896).

be imprudent. Therefore, the method of this
section is to introduce the reader to devotional literature by several of the more prominent Keswickian writers. A more extensive
list may be found in Barabas, SO GREAT SALVA-
TION.

From the preludes of Keswick, Hannah Whitall
Smith, THE CHRISTIAN'S SECRET OF A HAPPY LIFE
has retained popularity witnessed by the frequent reprintings by Revell. Early Keswick
leaders produced devotional literature of en-
during attraction: S. D. Gordon authored the
popular series, QUIET TALKS, at least 23 volumes, published by Revell; Alexander Smellie,
SERVICE AND INSPIRATION and THE WELL BY THE
WAY (London: Melrose, 1904 and 1920);
Charles A. Fox, VICTORY THROUGH THE NAME
(1894); and H. W. Webb-Peploe, "I FOLLOW AFT-
ER" (1894), WITHIN AND WITHOUT: OR, THE
CHRISTIAN'S FOES (1900), the last three published by Marshall Bros., and THE LIFE OF
PRIVILEGE, POSSESSION, PEACE, AND POWER (London: Nisbet, 1896).

H. C. G. Moule, the scholar, preacher, bishop,
produced CHRIST AND THE CHRISTIAN: WORDS
SPOKEN AT KESWICK (London: Marshall Bros.,
1919), THE CROSS AND THE SPIRIT (London: Seeley, 1898), and SECRET PRAYER (London: Seeley, 1890). Perhaps no one has been more influential in Keswickian spirituality, though
he spoke only once at the Convention, than Andrew Murray who wrote among other things, THE
MASTER'S INDWELLING, (1896) and THE INNER
CHAMBER AND THE INNER LIFE (1905) both by
Revell, THE SCHOOL OF OBEDIENCE (London: Nisbet, 1898), and ABIDE IN CHRIST: THOUGHTS ON
THE BLESSED LIFE OF FELLOWSHIP WITH THE SON
OF GOD (London: Nisbet, 1883). Many of Murray's works are being reprinted, as indicated
in recent editions of BOOKS IN PRINT.

F. B. Meyer, CHRISTIAN LIVING (London: Morgan & Scott, 1888), and THE DIRECTORY OF THE

DEVOUT LIFE: MEDITATIONS ON THE SERMON ON
THE MOUNT (New York: Revell, 1904), continue
to sustain interest while the once popular
writings of W. H. M. H. Aitken, especially
THE HIGHWAY OF HOLINESS: HELPS TO THE SPIRIT-
UAL LIFE (London: Shaw, 1883), unfortunately
do not. G. H. C. MacGregor, "RABBONI:" OR,
PERSONAL CONSECRATION (London: Marshall Bros.,
1904), and A HOLY LIFE AND HOW TO LIVE IT
(London: Marshall, Morgan & Scott, 1894),
are complements to the more erudite work of
an able scholar.

Jessie Penn-Lewis, of Welsh revival fame was
a popular author of devotional literature.
THE CROSS OF CALVARY AND ITS MESSAGE (London:
Marshall Bros., 1903), has gone through eight
editions, and OPENED HEAVENS (Parkstone: Overcomer Literature Trust, n.d.), has been recently reprinted.

The Fleming H. Revell Company published two
significant devotional series around the turn
of the century. LITTLE BOOKS FOR LIFE'S GUID-
ANCE included writings such as G. Campbell
Morgan, DISCIPLESHIP; Andrew Murray, THE
LORD'S TABLE; F. B. Meyer, SAVED AND KEPT,
COUNSELS TO YOUNG BELIEVERS, CHEER FOR LIFE'S
PILGRIMAGE; J. H. Barrows, I BELIEVE IN GOD
THE FATHER ALMIGHTY; and A. J. Gordon, YET
SPEAKING, UNPUBLISHED ADDRESSES. THE NORTH-
FIELD SERIES, addresses delivered at Moody's
Northfield Convention included G. Campbell
Morgan, THE TRUE ESTIMATE OF LIFE AND HOW TO
LIVE. Horatius Bonar, HOW SHALL I GO TO GOD
and GOD'S WAY OF PEACE, D. L. Moody, WEIGHED
AND WANTING: THE TEN COMMANDMENTS, as well
as other authors.

Amy Wilson Carmichael, the Keswick Convention's first missionary, continues to charm
Christian readers. EDGES OF HIS WAYS; SELEC-
TIONS FOR DAILY READING (London: S.P.C.K.,
1955); GOLD BY MOONLIGHT (London: S.P.C.K.,
1935); a book of meditations, IF... (London:

S.P.C.K., 1938); THOU GIVEST...THEY GATHER
(Fort Washington, Pa.: Christian Literature
Crusade, 1958); and the often reprinted WIN-
DOWS (London: S.P.C.K., 1937), are popular
devotional reading.

Devotional writings of other Keswick conven-
tioners are: Theodore Monod, THE GIFT OF GOD
(1876); W. Y. Fullerton, THE PRACTICE OF
CHRIST'S PRESENCE (1916), and GOD'S INTENTION
(1931); and Lionel B. Fletcher, AFTER CONVER-
SION - WHAT? (1936), all published by Marshall, Morgan & Scott, London; W. H. Griffith
Thomas, THE CHRISTIAN LIFE AND HOW TO LIVE IT
(Chicago: Moody, 1919); Gordon Watt, THE
CROSS IN FAITH AND CONDUCT (Philadelphia: Sunday School Times, 1922). Major W. Ian Thomas,
prominent in American and British Keswick circles, THE SAVING LIFE OF CHRIST (Grand Rapids:
Zondervan, 1961), is a popular study in the
atonement.

The American Keswickians were also prolific
writers of devotional literature. R. A. Tor-
rey, HOW TO SUCCEED IN THE CHRISTIAN LIFE
(1906), and REAL SALVATION AND WHOLEHEARTED
SERVICE (1905), as well as Robert Speer's ad-
dresses at Northfield, "REMEMBER JESUS CHRIST"
AND OTHER TALKS ABOUT CHRIST AND THE CHRIS-
TIAN LIFE (1899), were all published by Re-
vell. A. T. Pierson authored CATHARINE OF
SIENA, AN ANCIENT LAY PREACHER; A STORY OF
SANCTIFIED WOMANHOOD AND POWER IN PRAYER (New
York: Funk & Wagnalls, 1898), as well as the
more traditional THE BELIEVER'S LIFE: ITS
PAST, PRESENT, AND FUTURE TENSES (London:
Morgan & Scott, 1905).

James H. McConkey,[58] the founder of Silver

---

58. Louise Harrison McCraw, McConkey's long-
     time secretary, has written JAMES H. MC-
CONKEY, A MAN OF GOD (2nd ed., Grand Rapids:
Zondervan, 1939; reprinted Three Hills, Al-

Publishing Company, a non-profit press, pub-
lished THE THREE-FOLD SECRET OF THE HOLY SPIR-
IT, discussed above, and devotional tracts,
FAITH, GUIDANCE, CHASTENING, PRAYER, PRAYER
AND HEALING and GIVE GOD A CHANCE, all of
which are in print with Back to the Bible
Broadcast of Lincoln, Nebraska.

Stephen Olford, MANNA IN THE MORNING (1969)
and THE SECRET OF STRENGTH (1973)(Chicago:
Moody), the size of which belies their
influence, have had wide circulation. Alan
Redpath published sermons and abstracts of
sermons preached while he was pastor of Moody
Memorial Church, Chicago: LEARNING TO LIVE
(Grand Rapids: Eerdmans, 1961), and BLESS-
INGS OUT OF BUFFETINGS, STUDIES IN II CORIN-
THIANS (Westwood, N. J.: Revell, 1965).
Donald Grey Barnhouse, an American evangelist
who spoke several times at the Keswick Conven-
tion, wrote the popular GOD'S METHODS FOR
HOLY LIVING: PRACTICAL LESSONS IN EXPERIMEN-
TAL HOLINESS (London: Pickering & Inglis,
1937), THE INVISIBLE WAR (Grand Rapids: Zon-
dervan, 1965), and LIFE BY THE SON; PRACTICAL
LESSONS IN EXPERIMENTAL HOLINESS (Philadel-
phia: Revelation Publications, American Bible Conf. Assn., 1939).

Oswald J. Smith and the Christian and Missionary Alliance writers, Simpson and Tozer, contributed significantly to devotional literature in addition to their other works. Simpson wrote WALKING IN THE SPIRIT: THE HOLY
SPIRIT IN CHRISTIAN EXPERIENCE, (n.d.), THE
LIFE OF PRAYER, THE SELF LIFE AND THE CHRIST
LIFE (1097) and IN HEAVENLY PLACES (1892) all
by Christian Alliance Publishing Company and
currently available from Christian Publications, Harrisburg, Pa., as are over forty other volumes by this prolific author.

---

berta; Prairie Bible Institute, 1965).

Tozer, THE PURSUIT OF GOD (1948), THAT IN-
CREDIBLE CHRISTIAN (1964), and MAN, THE DWELL-
ING PLACE OF GOD (1966), are collections of
previously published devotional pieces (Har-
risburg, Christian Publications). Oswald J.
Smith contributed FROM DEATH TO LIFE, and THE
SPIRIT FILLED LIFE (New York: Christian Al-
liance, 1925 and 1926).

Catherine Marshall, BEYOND OURSELVES (1961)
consciously attempts to update the work of
Hannah Whitall Smith. SOMETHING MORE (1974)
is also an expression of higher life concerns.
Both are McGraw-Hill publications.

Present Keswick Convention leaders such as
Herbert F. Stevenson, THE ROAD TO THE CROSS
(London: Marshall, Morgan & Scott, 1963), A
GALAXY OF SAINTS (Revell, 1958), and John R.
W. Stott, CONFESS YOUR SINS (Phila.: Westmin-
ster, 1964), MEN MADE NEW: AN EXPOSITION OF
ROMANS 5-8 (London: Inter-Varsity, 1966),
and CHRIST THE LIBERATOR (London: Hodder &
Stoughton, 1972), are continuing in the Kes-
wick tradition.

This presentation of the Keswickian tradition
of spirituality indicates the diversity and
yet the sameness of the concern. There is
little change - merely, although importantly,
a re-stating of emphases for the Keswick au-
dience and the Christian world.

Hymnody

The hymnody of the Keswick Convention has,
for all practical purposes, been ignored. F.
S. Webster, "Keswick Hymns," in THE KESWICK
CONVENTION, ITS MESSAGE, ITS METHOD AND ITS
MEN, edited by Charles F. Harford, is long on
glowing description and void of concrete analysis.

Initially Robert Pearsall Smith, HYMNS SELECT-
ED FROM FABER (Boston: Willard Tract Reposi-

tory; London: W. Isbister, 1874), without
music, was received widely. This was replac-
ed by HYMNS OF CONSECRATION AND FAITH: FOR
USE AT GENERAL CHRISTIAN CONFERENCES, MEET-
INGS FOR THE DEEPENING OF SPIRITUAL LIFE AND
CONSECRATION MEETINGS,compiled and arranged
by Rev. J. Mountain (n.d.), of which a second edition, new and enlarged was compiled
by Mrs. Evan Hopkins (1895), both published
by Marshall Brothers. THE KESWICK HYMN-BOOK
compiled by the Trustees of the Keswick Convention (London: Marshall, Morgan & Scott,
n.d.),was published in the 1930's, followed
in 1938 by an enlarged edition. Amy Carmichael published WINGS: A BOOK OF DOHNAVUR
SONGS (London: S.P.C.K., 1960-).

In America, A. J. Gordon compiled THE VESTRY
HYMN AND TUNE BOOK (Boston: Young, 1872).
Moody's movement gave strength to American
hymnody and gospel song but produced little
that was distinctive. The Christian and Mis-
sionary Alliance, led by Simpson, HYMNS AND
SONGS OF THE FOURFOLD GOSPEL, AND THE FULLNESS
OF JESUS (New York: Christian Alliance,
1891), without music, and HYMNS OF THE CHRIS-
TIAN LIFE; NEW AND STANDARD SONGS FOR THE
SANCTUARY, SUNDAY SCHOOLS, PRAYER MEETINGS,
MISSION WORK AND REVIVAL SERVICES, ed. Capt.
R. Kelso Carter and Rev. A. B. Simpson (New
York: Christian Alliance, 1891), with music,
has since moved to a more traditional hymnal,
basically indistinguishable from those of oth-
er denominations, HYMNS OF THE CHRISTIAN LIFE;
A BOOK OF WORSHIP IN SONG EMPHASIZING EVAN-
GELISM, MISSIONS AND THE DEEPER LIFE, 1936
(revised and enlarged, 1962).

Periodicals: England

THE CHRISTIAN, A WEEKLY RECORD OF CHRISTIAN
LIFE, CHRISTIAN TESTIMONY AND CHRISTIAN WORK
(London) 1870-1969. Here were reported the
Brighton and Oxford conferences as Figgis
and E. Hopkins contributed summaries. Other

meetings of the Robert Pearsall Smiths received coverage as did those of Moody. There is not a complete file in the United States. From 1962 to 1969 published by The Billy Graham Evangelistic Association as THE CHRISTIAN AND CHRISTIANITY TODAY.

THE CHRISTIAN'S PATHWAY TO POWER, 1874-1878. Founded by Robert Pearsall Smith, it was, after his downfall, taken up by W. E. Boardman and then by Evan H. Hopkins. It became THE LIFE OF FAITH.

THE LIFE OF FAITH (London), 1878-   Formerly THE CHRISTIAN'S PATHWAY TO POWER, it was supervised by Evan Hopkins, although initially edited by Charles Grandison Moore. The editorship has remained in the hands of Keswickians, and the paper remains an unofficial voice of the Keswick Convention. No complete file has been found.

KESWICK WEEK, 1892-   The addresses delivered at the Keswick Convention have been published since 1892 under various titles. Except for the war years (1940?-1945) when these appeared as KESWICK IN LONDON or similar titles, the caption was KESWICK WEEK or KESWICK CONVENTION. Reports of conferences 1875-1891 appeared in THE LIFE OF FAITH or its predecessor THE CHRISTIAN'S PATHWAY TO POWER.

SOUTH AFRICAN PIONEER (London) 1- , 1887-

Periodicals: America

NORTHFIELD ECHOES (East Northfield, Mass.) 1-10 (1894-1903). Authors included J. W. Chapman, A. J. Gordon, Mrs. Gordon, T. S. Hamlin, F. B. Meyer, Moody, A. T. Pierson, R. A. Torrey and D. W. and M. J. Whittle.

MOODY CHURCH HERALD, (Chicago) 1902, 1903. Included articles by and about Moody, R. A.

Torrey, W. W. White and A. T. Pierson.

RECORD OF CHRISTIAN WORK (East Northfield,
Mass.; 1-18 New York: Revell). 1-52 (1881-
1933). Reports on the activities of Hannah
Whitall Smith, Moody and Sankey, Andrew Murray and H. W. Webb-Peploe. Important are F.
B. Meyer "The New Life," v. 14 (1895), 198-
199 and H. W. Webb-Peploe "The True Unity of
the Church," v. 15 (1896), 224-225. In April
1904 it absorbed NORTHFIELD ECHOES.

THE INSTITUTE TIE (Chicago) 1: 1-24 Nov. 7,
1891- Oct. 30, 1892; 2: 1-6, Nov. 15,
1892-Feb. 15, 1893. N.S. 1-10, 1900/01-1910.
Here were published notes of R. A. Torrey's
lectures at the Bible Institute as well as
reports of the Moody-Sankey tours of Europe.
The subtitle of the magazine varies. Complete file at Moody Bible Institute, Chicago.
It became THE CHRISTIAN WORKERS MAGAZINE.

CHRISTIAN WORKERS MAGAZINE (Chicago). Octo-
ber, 1910-August, 1920. Complete file at
Moody Bible Institute, Chicago. It became
MOODY BIBLE INSTITUTE MONTHLY.

MOODY BIBLE INSTITUTE MONTHLY (Chicago).
1920-1938. Complete file at Moody Bible Institute, Chicago. It became MOODY MONTHLY.

MOODY MONTHLY (Chicago). 1938- Complete file at Moody Bible Institute, Chicago.

THE MID-AMERICA KESWICK WEEK (Chicago). 1959.
Only one published. Includes addresses by
Alan Redpath, Stephen Olford, C. S. Woods,
Paul Rees, Ian Thomas, Allister Smith, Arthur
Matthews, H. Wildish and William Culbertson
delivered at Moody Memorial Church.

MISSIONARY REVIEW OF THE WORLD (Brooklyn,
N.Y.) 1878-1939. 1878-1887 was published as
MISSIONARY REVIEW. Edited by A. T. Pierson.
While there are no complete files, such could

be compiled. See UNION LIST OF
2692.

THE OVERCOMER (London: Bournemouth) 1909-
1914; 1920-1948. Product of the Welsh revival era, edited by Mrs. Jessie Penn-Lewis.

ADVOCATE OF CHRISTIAN HOLINESS (Boston) 1-13,
1870-1881. An American Holiness Movement
journal whose British correspondent, W. G.
Pascoe reported work of Smiths, etc. in a
column entitled, "Work of Holiness in England".
Published briefly, 1882, as ADVOCATE OF BIBLE
HOLINESS.

SOUTH AFRICAN PIONEER, American ed. (Brooklyn,
N.Y.) 1-   (Dec. 1920-   ). Aug./Sept. 1941,
merged with British edition.

Periodicals: Christian and Missionary Alliance

THE WORD, THE WORK, AND THE WORLD (New York)
1887. It became CHRISTIAN ALLIANCE AND FOR-
EIGN MISSIONARY WEEKLY.

CHRISTIAN ALLIANCE AND FOREIGN MISSIONARY
WEEKLY. 1887-1896. It became CHRISTIAN AND
MISSIONARY ALLIANCE.

CHRISTIAN AND MISSIONARY ALLIANCE. 1897-
Sept. 1911. It became ALLIANCE WEEKLY.

ALLIANCE WEEKLY. Oct. 1911-Dec. 25, 1957.
It became ALLIANCE WITNESS.

ALLIANCE WITNESS. 1957-   . Note: Volumes
24-34 are repeated in numbering.

NAME INDEX

A

Abbott, J. J., 17
Aitken, W. H., 58, 77
Alexander, Charles, 38
Allen, R. W., 14
Arthur, William, 15, 18, 57

B

Baird, John, 55
Baldwin, H. A., 45
Barabas, Steven, 18, 26, 34, 38, 39, 55, 57, 76
Baring-Gould, S., 11
Barnhouse, D. G., 67, 79
Barrows, J. H., 77
Battersby, T. D. Harford, 24, 26, 32, 34, 55, 60
Baxter, J. S., 61
Baxter, Mrs. M., 29
Bennett, Lucy, 62
Blackwood, S. A., 74, 23, 74, 75
Boardman, H. A., 17
Boardman, W. E., 16, 17, 18, 20, 22, 27, 30, 36, 50, 54, 57, 82
Bonar, Horatius, 12, 77
Bowker, H. F., 20, 24
Brandenburg, H., 31
Brash, John, 14
Brockett, H. E., 46
Brooke, Hubert, 62, 71
Broomhall, Marshall, 33

Buckland, A. R., 73

C

Carmichael, Amy, 33, 77, 81
Carter, R. K., 81
Cattell, Everett, 47
Caughey, James, 14, 15, 16
Chapman, J. W., 82
Cooke, Sarah, 37
Cowper-Temple, W., 19, 20
Croome, T. M., 24
Culbertson, William, 66, 83
Cumming, J. E., 58
Dale, A. W. W., 57
Dale, R. W., 57, 64
Dayton, D. W., 13, 42, 45, 46, 47, 69
Dieter, M. E., 12, 15, 19, 27, 30, 47, 48
Dixon, A. C., 53, 71
Douglas, J. D., 57
Douglas, W. M., 40
Douglass, P. F., 31
Dowie, Alexander, 48
Drummond, A. L., 31
Dunn, L. R., 70
Du Plessis, J., 40

E

Ehlert, A. D., 64
Ekvall, R. B., 51
Evans, Eifion, 29

F

Failing, G. E., 47
Fairchild, J. H., 12, 13
Faupel, D. W., 42, 48, 69

Figgis, J. B., 26, 81

Findlay, J. F., 37

Finney, C. G., 13, 14, 16, 30

Fishbourne, E. G., 63

Fleisch, Paul, 30, 31

Fletcher, L. B., 78

Fletcher, John, 12

Fletcher, R. S., 12

Fox, C. A., 62, 74, 76

Fullerton, W. Y., 39, 78

G

Garrard, Mary, 30

Garrison, S. D., 69

Gathorne-Hardy, R., 22

Geiger, Kenneth, 47

Getz, G. A., 37

Glover, R. H., 50

Godbey, W. B., 43, 48

Goodman, George, 74

Goodspeed, E. J., 36

Gordon, A. J., 40, 48, 49, 50, 63, 68, 73, 77, 81, 82

Gordon, Mrs. A. J., 82

Gordon, E. B., 50

Gordon, S. D., 63, 76

Gray, J. M., 50

Guinness, M. Geraldine, 33

Guyon, Madame, 12, 15

H

Hall, John, 36

Hamilton, Sir Wm., 14

Harford, Charles F., 12, 34, 62, 80

Harford, John, 60

Harries, John, 40

Harris, J. R., 21

Hay, A. M., 34

Head, Albert, 28

Hefley, J. C. 51

Hills, A. M., 13, 44, 46, 48

Hitt, R. T., 51

Holden, J. S., 33, 60, 64

Hopkins, E. H., 14, 22, 23, 25, 26, 28, 56, 58, 60, 62, 81, 82

Hopkins, Mrs. E. H., 81

Houghton, Frank, 33

Houghton, W., 62

Hunter, J. H., 51

I

Ibister, W., 81

Inwood, Charles, 34

Ironside, H. A., 46, 52, 66, 74

J

Jackson, Edna, 20

Jellinghaus, Theodor, 31, 32

Johnson, E. H., 26

Jones, Charles, 25, 39, 42, 43, 45, 46, 52, 70

Jones, Cynddylan, 28

Jones, D. C., 63

Jones, R. B., 28

Jüngst, Johannes, 19

K

King, L. L., 51

Kropatscheck, F. D., 19

L

Laidlaw, John, 57
Latourette, K. S., 35
Law, William, 12
Lawrence, Brother, 12
Lloyd-Jones, D. M., 61

M

McCheyne, R. M., 12
McConkey, J. H., 66, 78
McCrossan, T. J., 68
Macdonald, F. C., 55
MacDonald, George, 20
Macfarlane, N. C., 35
McGraw, James, 44
McGraw, Louise, 78
MacGregor, D. C., 59
MacGregor, G. H. R., 59, 62, 73, 77
MacKenzie, Kenneth, 50
Maclean, J. K., 28, 38
McLoughlin, W. G., 13
McQuilkin, R. C., 66, 74
Mahan, Asa, 13, 14, 16, 18, 22, 30, 36, 37, 43, 54, 57, 64
Mantle, J. G., 50
Marshall, Catherine, 80
Marshall, Walter, 12, 54
Matthews, Arthur, 83
Matthews, David, 29
Melrose, Andrew, 56

Menzies, William, 48
Meyer, F. B., 28, 29, 34, 36, 39, 41, 49, 52, 59, 60, 62, 70, 74, 76, 77, 82, 83
Meyer, Louis, 53
Miller, B. W., 18
Mitchell, Fred, 23, 26, 33
Modersohn, Ernst, 31
Monod, Theodore, 20, 21, 23, 78
Moody, D. L., 16, 34, 36, 37, 38, 65, 71, 77, 82, 83
Moody, P. D., 36
Moody, W. R., 36
Moore, C. G., 14, 28, 33, 62, 82
Moore, E. W., 25, 62
Morgan, G. C., 36, 39, 40, 41, 59, 64, 73, 75, 77
Morgan, Jill, 40
Morgan, J. V., 29
Morton, A. Q., 73
Moule, H. C. G., 11, 24, 26, 54, 55, 56, 58, 60, 62, 64, 73, 76
Mountain, J., 81
Mudge, James, 69, 70
Müller, George, 12, 18
Murray, Andrew, 39, 40, 54, 59, 63, 76, 77, 83
Murray, Harold, 41

N

Needham, Helen, 67, 72
Neill, Stephen, 32
Nugent, Sophia, 62

O

Olford, Stephen, 79, 83

Orr, J. E., 15, 16, 29
Overton, J. H., 11

Rober
Ruther   12
Ryle, J. C., 61

P
Pache, René, 67, 71
Padwick, Constance, 34
Page, I. E., 14
Palmer, Phoebe, 14, 16
Palmer, W. C., 16
Pardington, G. P., 50, 51, 67, 69
Pascoe, W. G., 84
Paynter, F., 28
Peck, Gregory, 15
Penn-Lewis, Jessie, 28, 29, 30, 57, 63, 77, 84
Pentecost, J. D., 67
Phelps, A. A., 70
Phillips, T., 24
Pierson, A. T., 18, 25, 28, 38, 50, 52, 57, 62, 71, 72, 73, 74, 78, 82, 83
Pierson, D. L., 25
Pollock, J. C., 27, 29, 31, 32, 33, 34, 35, 36, 56, 62
Poole, Richard, 18
Pusey, E. B., 10

R
Radcliffe, Reginald, 32
Rader, Paul, 50
Rappard, Heinrich, 31
Redpath, Alan, 79, 83

S
Sandeen, E. R., 41, 64, 66
Sankey, I. D., 16, 36, 37, 83
Schmul, H. E., 45
Scofield, C. I., 65, 66
Scroggie, W. G., 61, 64, 71, 72, 73
Scroggie, Mrs. J. J., 72
Senft, F. H., 50, 67
Shaw, S. B., 29
Shipley, Murray, 24
Short, A. R., 18
Simpson, A. B., 48, 49, 50, 52, 67, 68, 73, 79, 81
Sloan, W. B., 25
Smellie, Alexander, 23, 56, 58, 76
Smith, Allister, 83
Smith, Amanda, 20, 21, 28, 36
Smith, F. W., 19, 21
Smith, G. B., 75
Smith, Hannah W., 18, 19, 21, 22, 76, 80, 83
Smith, L. P., 18, 19, 22
Smith, O. J., 52, 67, 68, 69, 79, 80
Smith, R. P., 16, 18, 19, 20, 21, 27, 30, 36, 54, 74, 80, 82, 83
Smith, Thornley, 14

Smith, Timothy, 15
Smith, W. M., 37,
  67, 69
Speer, R. E., 34,
  35
Steele, Daniel, 45,
  70
Stevenson, H. F.,
  27, 57, 63, 74,
  75, 80
Stewart, Herbert,
  64
Stock, Eugene, 32,
  34
Stockmayer, Otto,
  31, 32
Stoesz, S. J., 51
Stott, J. R. W.,
  74, 80
Strachey, Ray, 22
Street, M. Jennie,
  39
Synan, Vincent, 42

T

Taylor, Mrs. F. H.
  see Guinness M.
  Geraldine
Taylor, J. H., 33
Taylor, M. W., 21
Taylor, William, 59
Thomas à Kempis, 12
Thomas, W. I., 78,
  83
Thomas, W. H. G.,
  12, 56, 60, 71,
  72, 73, 75, 78
Thompson, A. E., 50
Thompson, Phyllis,
  33, 34
Thompson, W. R., 47
Thornton, G. R., 24
Tiesmayer, L., 31
Todd, J. A., 17
Torrey, R. A., 29,
38, 52, 53, 65, 71,
  72, 78, 82, 83
Tozer, A. W., 50, 51,
  52, 67, 68, 75, 79,
  80
Turnbull, W. M., 50

U

Upham, Thomas, 15, 27,
  30

W

Warfield, B. B., 15, 17,
  19, 27, 31
Warren, W. F., 70
Watt, Gordon, 78
Wayland, Francis, 18
Webb-Peploe, H. W.,
  23, 24, 25, 38, 60,
  64, 76, 83
Webster, F. S., 62, 80
Wentz, A. R., 31
Wesley, John, 12, 47
Westcott, B. F., 55
Wheeler, W. R., 34
White, W. W., 83
Whittle, D. W., 82
Whittle, M. J., 82
Wilberforce, Canon (A.
  B. O.), 21
Wildish, H., 83
Wilcy, H. O., 44
Wilson, Robert, 24
Winkler, Fr., 19, 30
Wise, Daniel, 14, 15
Woods, C. S., 83
Wrenford, J. T., 62
Wright, James, 18

Z

Zikmund, Barbara, 13

www.ingramcontent.com/pod-product-compliance
Lightning Source LLC
Chambersburg PA
CBHW020513030426
42337CB00011B/369